The 1954 version of the A6GCS illustrates the model's excellent proportions. Note the screen (protects the driver only) and the grille design. Many Italian sports car drivers cut their teeth on this popular competition Maserati. Today, this Maserati is highly sought after and is rarely available on the open market.

Illustrated

Maserati
BUYER'S GUIDE™

Second Edition

Richard Crump & Rob de la Rive Box

Motorbooks International
Publishers & Wholesalers ®

CREDITS AND ACKNOWLEDGMENTS

Both Richard Crump and Rob de la Rive Box wish to express their thanks to the following individuals and organizations who contributed photographs and information: Officine Alfieri Maserati S.p.A., Carrozzeria Bertone, Pinin Farina, Ital Design, Egon Hofer, Alexis Callier, Corrado Millanta and material used from the collection of the late Hans Tanner.

The publisher wishes to acknowledge the observations of Maserati's American scene given by John Ratto and Joe Benson.

This edition published in 1989 by Motorbooks International Publishers & Wholesalers, P O Box 2, 729 Prospect Avenue, Osceola, WI 54020 USA

© Richard Crump and Rob de la Rive Box, 1989

First published in 1984

Motorbooks International books are also available at discounts in bulk quantity for industrial or sales-promotional use. For details write to Special Sales Manager at the Publisher's address

Library of Congress Cataloging-in-Publication Data
Crump, Richard
    Illustrated Maserati buyer's guide / Richard Crump & Rob de la Rive Box.—2nd ed.
      p. cm.
    Bibliography: p.
    ISBN 0-87938-396-8
    1. Maserati automobile—Purchasing.
I. Rive Box, Rob de la.
II. Title.
TL215.M34C76 1989   89-12537
629.222'2—dc20   CIP

On the front cover: 1970 Maserati Gibli Spyder AM115.S.1169. Photograph by Francis G. Mandarano, taken with a Mamiya 2¼x2¾ RB67 Pro S using Fujichrome 100 color transparency film.

On the back cover: The Karif as first seen at Geneva in 1988 with a 2.8 liter V-6, twin water-cooled turbos and double intercooler.

Printed and bound in the United States of America

TABLE OF CONTENTS

PREFACE

Following her defeat at Wimbledon in 1983, tennis star Virginia Wade said of her victor, "Martina Navratilova is like a Ferrari among saloons this year." Whether or not Miss Wade has a Ferrari is irrelevant; that the word obviously comes easier to her mind than Maserati is important. The same can be said of many people unassociated with motor cars, and if a cross section of the public were interviewed it is likely a large proportion would have heard of Ferrari and possibly would think that a Maserati is either a pizza or a pop group.

Certainly there are differences between these two great Italian marques, but they are not definable. My opinion of why Ferrari is better known or is more easily recalled is that it participates in Grand Prix racing, a sport which receives worldwide coverage through all media.

The Rampant Horse never let go of Formula One, whereas Maserati retired on its 1957 laurels never to emerge as a serious challenger in the top echelons of the sport. It is unlikely that DeTomaso will have the necessary financial funding to enter any form of single-seater racing, although it is known he retains an interest in the sport. Besides a private Italian effort with a competition Biturbo, there is little to represent the trident on today's racetracks.

Maybe in truth there is no mystique attached to either Maserati or Ferrari and the universal following that both enjoy is unfairly exploited by owners of the cars. Whatever you feel for either of these great car constructors, a feeling will emerge stronger for one than the other, and in the final analysis that emotion will dictate your enthusiasm.

Richard Crump
Rob de la Rive Box

INTRODUCTION

Many motorists, at one time or another during their more enthusiastic years, have a desire to own an Italian automobile. For them, the dream is not which make but how soon they can turn their dream into reality. It has proved quite an easy task to acquire the Italian car; the difficulty has, in many cases, been rebuilding, restoring or simply maintaining the animal in the style in which it was conceived. Whether one sees oneself in a tiny Fiat 500 weaving spaghetti lines in and out of busy traffic (which can be fun) or cruising the highways at a limit that the exotic will embrace in first gear, is basically irrelevant. The matter is strictly confined to owning and living with the Italian car, a feat which many achieve with full heart and light wallet, feeling psychologically superior to their friends and neighbors.

The number of motor cars available from an Italian factory is great, so remember that the year of manufacture is important, for that conveys to you the era which you associate with or the trend in automobile design that has the most appeal. Similar to good wine being "laid down" for a number of years in order to enhance its bouquet, so some Italian automobiles gain in charm, quality and, naturally, value. But like the wine, the car must be looked after and not allowed to appear down at the heel or shabby in any way. A friend of mine with a 1959 Maserati 3500GT coupe likens it to his wife's Steinway concert grand, and they both use their possessions with equal respect and regularity. If the Italian car you aspire to own is a Maserati, then I hope this book will encourage that aspiration, for that is one of the reasons it is being written.

To purchase a Maserati, one should gain access to the model's world-famous grapevine. I use the phrase "world famous" since the relatively low volume output from this Modenese factory during the postwar period makes Maserati owners a practical-size family although scattered worldwide. Up until the seventies no club or association existed for this marque, but in 1971 a Maserati club was founded in England by Richard Crump. Since that time clubs in Sweden, France, Germany, Switzerland, Australia and the USA have been formed with good effect. Each in its own way contributes greatly to the ownership of cars bearing Neptune's Trident.

Aside from the clubs, motor magazines carrying classified advertisements frequently offer examples for sale or trade. Money spent during two or three months on such literature will give you a relative idea of the movement and price of Maseratis. You will also want to invest in the one-make books, which will not prove financially crippling since there are still only a few Maserati histories in publication.

Assuming you have actually made the basic choice between a spyder or a coupe, you must then choose between two engine designs: the in-line six-cylinder or the V-8. Both power units have a lot to recommend them, but with the V-8 comes a new era of coachwork styles and that is where your eye becomes the master. Generally, the six-cylinder cars have a larger following in Europe and Australia, the V-8's in the USA and Scandinavia. The sixes owe their heritage to the Grand Prix and sports racing cars up to 1958 and the eight-cylinders to the rumbling 450S sports racers and some later Le Mans attempts. Of course, the factory did make four-cylinder cars, but these were all competition machines commencing with the 150S and closing with the rear-engine Birdcages. We have purposely confined comment and observations on the competition Maseratis to the final chapters.

Remember that Maserati did make some of its models with right-hand-drive steering for the UK and Australian consumers. It would be rare for a right-hand-drive model to be offered for sale on the American market. A strange animal such as this would probably have a low resale value owing to its alien environment.

After you have acquainted yourself with the various models to be considered, a telephone conversation or visit with an owner can prove invaluable. While his motives for ownership may not coincide with your own, it is unlikely that he will mislead you about a common interest.

When investigating a possible purchase you may note the "I" which can follow the model designation, this represents inezione, or injection, which means the engine is fitted with a fuel-metering unit made by Lucas in England.

There is a good deal of controversy regarding maintenance of the Lucas fuel-injection system. The authors feel that this setup should be retained, rebuilt if necessary, and cared for properly. But we do realize that these systems have their faults. If a fuel-injected car has been stored for a length of time, the rubber sealing gaskets can dry out and shrink, resulting in cylinder wear and bearing problems caused by excess fuel. More serious, perhaps, are the difficulties encountered on the 100 psi fuel pumps. Prior to 1967 these units were subject to failure due to a lack of lubrication. Units since 1967 have a device that corrects this problem and these fuel distributors are reliable. Any unit with many miles on it probably should be rebuilt.

Another alternative is going to carburetors. In 1970 the Maserati Information Exchange developed a kit for converting the six-cylinder engines to a three-Weber setup which costs about $1,000. Owners who have made this conversion have been pleased with the results and many believe the Webers are a better choice than the Lucas fuel injection. There is, however, the likelihood that horsepower will drop with carburetors, and they will also cause the engine to run dirtier.

Converting to carbs may not drastically reduce the car's value since there is precedence for the Webers, so many have been changed over and there will always be a number of buyers who are intimidated by fuel injection anyway. But we hasten to add that Webers on a post-1962 six-cylinder Maserati are not authentic and there are ways of rebuilding and caring for the correct Lucas system. The units are very much a specialist item, but once overhauled and calibrated correctly will run trouble-free and economically. Except for the 5000GT the V-8's were all equipped with Weber carburetors and, generally speaking, overhaul kits and jets are available.

Maserati fitted only Borrani wheels to its six-cylinder and early V-8 models, going later to Campagnolo light alloy. The Borrani wire wheels had seventy-two spokes; the solid Borrani had steel centers with riveted aluminum rims all originally wearing Pirelli rubber. If a Maserati has wire wheels, they were almost certainly fitted by the factory before delivery to the car's first owner or distributor. Wire wheels corrode, are a maintenance headache and expensive to rebuild but are certainly beautiful. The sixteen-inch tires are available from Dunlop, Pirelli and Avon.

The engine in either form can be expensive to totally rebuild, but once done correctly will run up to 50,000 miles on regular maintenance. The word "totally" means exactly what it conveys; at this writing, the price for replacing literally every single item on an in-line-six road car engine is around $15,000, while a V-8 would be closer to $19,000. A rebuild replacing only worn parts would run $8,000 to $10,000.

Regular servicing can be done by nearly anyone, with the possible exception of tuning the Webers or adjusting the fuel injection. On the injection engines, a straight 50-grade oil should be used and changed every 2,400 miles; the viscosity of this oil helps combat contamination from the fuel system. Oil changes to transmission and axle are as the manual instructs. The remaining care and attention is no more or less than you would do to your everyday vehicle. Obviously, a complete range of metric tools will be necessary. Generally speaking you will find that Maserati engines have higher torque and run at fewer rpm than other exotics. They are, therefore, somewhat easier to drive and probably will require less maintenance.

The transmissions were consigned to Maserati by ZF in Germany beginning with a four-speed version in 1958 and then fitting a five-speed in 1961 and 1962. These gearboxes were extremely well made and merely require the driver's tolerance while changing from first to second gear when the engine is cold. The units benefit from regular oil changes.

The rear axle has never been known to give any kind of problem and was originally built by Salisbury in the UK.

The brakes were Girling, while the disc was actually manufactured by Maserati to its own specification.

The chassis and coachwork were unable to hide any defects by virtue of their construction. If the oval-tube chassis has ever been involved in an accident it will show with creases in the tubing near the firewall (bulkhead) or around the steel footwells, and can easily be seen from the underside. If the symptoms are there, walk away from the car, regardless of the price, since jig repairs on the chassis are very expensive.

Italian coachwork is renowned for its style but not necessarily its construction. Whether the body was built of aluminum or steel or a combination of both, it was given a considerable helping of "stucco" to contour the sharp edges and smooth the line (especially bodies from Frua and Touring). Whatever the composite of the original Italian filler, its removal is akin to separating concrete from a wall of bricks. The only satisfactory method is with a chemical solvent. But before resorting to those fearsome procedures, realize that correct preparation and a high-quality repaint will work effectively without stripping to bare metal. Do not worry, Maserati was not the only manufacturer to use this type of Bondo.

The factory had many well-known coachbuilders construct its bodies; yet, strangely, the more desirable convertible models were executed in steel (perhaps for the increased torsional rigidity). Aluminum bodies were also wrapped around steel hoops, so corrosion where the two different metals touch *and* encounter water can be a problem. A galvanic reaction occurs which oxidizes the aluminum—even a small pinhole where the aluminum has been sacrificed will cause paint to bubble. Your best bet is to keep this from happening by making sure these areas (particularly the lip around the wheel wells) are sealed from moisture.

External fittings used by Maserati were of proprietary Italian manufacture, the only suspect piece being the bumpers, which, unless stainless steel as on some early 3500's, always need repair and quality rechroming.

American enthusiast Joe Benson made up the following list of pitfalls to watch for when buying:

Ensure that engine and gearbox are in reasonable operating condition to avoid major expenses.

It may be difficult-to-impossible to replace missing trim since so many items were hand formed, filed and custom fit to each car. Trim from a parts car may be unusable. In fact, most trim pieces are stamped with the chassis number (for originality buffs).

Aluminum bodywork requires a much higher skill level to repair than steel.

Custom fabrication may be required to replace the soft tops of the roadster models.

Don't buy an older Maser with a broken or cracked windshield unless you're fairly sure of a replacement.

On the road, the six-cylinder cars are wonderfully long-legged, the engine will sing all day long at 120 mph, and the roadholding is sensitive only if the road gets wet. Once at a high cruising speed, one can play tunes with the gearbox, any transmission whine will be long gone. Think of flexing your muscles in the corners, since the luxury of power steering was not fitted on these models. Fuel economy is actually quite good.

The V-8 Maseratis are, as you would expect, considerably different to drive. Whether your purchase is a front- or mid-engine layout, both will propel you in a sophisticated, untiring fashion—and that five-liter power unit can put your mind in heaven. Use the engine in every gear; make it climb the rev counter into the red zone with every change, and you will begin to realize what life was like for the test drivers on those rapid autostradas. Have no fears of bursting the engine or putting a rod through the side of the block, since both engines are, if anything, understressed. The V-8's fuel consumption is fairly high, but they may be the smoothest, nicest sounding of all V-8 engines.

Unlike the Ferraris, Maseratis are extremely civilized cars to live with on an everyday basis. They don't overheat or foul plugs in rush hour traffic, and are quite docile in spite of their high power output and top speed potential. This unfussy nature makes Maseratis particularly desirable in speed-limited America.

Owning a Maserati is living with a legend that was created in 1926 by a family of brothers. For almost sixty years every type of formula, sports and road model has at one time been produced by the company in both prewar Bologna and Modena since 1946.

The emotional experience of ownership is worth the search and, hopefully, the acquisition. With a Maserati you will always feel related to a very personal and historic car constructor. And remember, a high percentage of Maserati owners possess not one but two of these creations, so you are not stepping into an unknown world by yourself.

NUMBERING SYSTEM

The first Maseratis built and sold after World War II were given serial numbers for both chassis and engine. Each was stamped by the factory and records kept pertaining to its original specification, purchaser's name, country of destination and date the car went through the factory gates. Later, a printed plate was riveted to the firewall, and stamped with both serial numbers. In many instances these plates became souvenirs for original or later owners which is very annoying.

The first production Maserati cars were not built until 1958-59 and were all given the prefix AM. Those two letters represent the initials of the founder of the company Alfieri Maserati, and are retained today on all chassis plates which are to be found beneath the hood. The location of Maserati serial numbers varied considerably in each model up to the seventies after which some regularity emerged. In rare instances the number is missing.

The front-engine production cars were marked on top of the wishbone near the leading exhaust pipe; the mid-engine cars, on one of the square tubes within the engine compartment. In each case, engines were stamped at the rear where the bellhousing for the clutch and gearbox locates.

On competition cars, frankly, the serial numbers can be anywhere. Many of these chassis had numbered plates spot-welded onto the front chassis cross-member which was the factory style up to the end of 1959. Engines invariably were stamped in the valley between each camshaft, at the rear of the block or above the front leg casting.

You can be almost 100 percent certain that *somewhere* the Maserati will be marked with an identification number. If your Maserati is to be used for your exclusive enjoyment, the serial number may not be important to you. However, if you are buying one of the competition models make sure that the frame and engine carry bona fide identification, otherwise the historical significance of the car will be per-

Identification plate from a 3500GT.

manently in doubt. Genuine documentation for Maseratis that have had any sort of competition life is imperative, and will greatly affect the future sale.

The identification digits used by the Maserati factory are as follows:

A - Alfieri
C - Corsa
F - Formula
G - Ghisa
I - International
M - Monoposto
S - Sport

Significant tipo (type) numbers are:

6 - number of cylinders
8 - number of cylinders
150 - 1½ liters
200 - two liters
250 - 2½ liters
300 - three liters
350 - 3½ liters
450 - 4½ liters

So, an identification plate bearing the numbers 250F is on a 2½-liter formula car, in this instance a Grand Prix racing car. After the tipo (type) number will appear the build number—for example, 2529, or the twenty-ninth car in that series. Similarly, an A6G/2000 will be a six-cylinder, two-liter car and the number 2012 will represent the twelfth car in that series.

Dating a Maserati can, in some cases, be difficult since it may require access to factory archives which is not permitted. On models imported into the USA from Italy a source of dating can be the seller's files, or the licensing authorities. But remember that there will be a slight discrepancy in the month, owing to the time lag involved between the car leaving Modena and its arrival at the port of entry.

Once again, this is an area where period magazine articles, books and general research will pay dividends.

MODEL DESIGNATIONS

Maserati designated each production car with a typo, or type, number, and in some cases with a name. The derivation of each model name is as follows:

Sebring - named after the factory's competition association with this famous American racing circuit.

Mistral - a northwest wind blowing from land to sea in the Gulf of Leone on the French Mediterranean coast.

Quattroporte - a four-door.

Mexico - to commemorate John Surtees' winning of the 1966 Mexican Grand Prix driving a Cooper Maserati.

Ghibli - a collection of winds blowing across the Sahara desert.

Indy - to commemorate the winning of the Indianapolis 500-mile race in 1939 and 1940 by a Maserati type 8CTF.

Bora - a particularly strong north-by-northwest wind blowing from land toward the north Adriatic sea.

Merak - the second star of the constellation of the Plough.

Khamsin - a hot, violent gale which blows across the Sahara each year. The gale can last up to two months at a time.

Preceding each serial number on the identification plate of the production models you will find the letters AM followed by the designated type number for the model. This is simply explained by listing the tipo numbers as follows:

AM/101 - 3500 series
AM/101/10 - Sebring or 3500GTIS series
AM/109 - Mistral series
AM/103 - 5000GT series
AM/107 - first Quattroporte series
AM/112 - Mexico
AM/115 - Ghibli
AM/116 - Indy
AM/117 - Bora
AM/122 - Merak
AM/120 - Khamsin
AM/330 - second Quattroporte series and Royale
AM/331 - Biturbo

If the letter S is used with any of the above it means spyder, or convertible; the letter A represents four-liter and is applicable only to six-cylinder cars. A capacity change on V-8 models would be indicated as 47 (4700 cc) or 49 (4900 cc).

It can be confusing, but once you have actually seen a chassis plate the numbers will become surprisingly simple to understand.

INVESTMENT RATINGS

★★★★★ The best. The highest price coupled to the best possibility of further appreciation. The days of finding these cars through magazine advertisements have long gone; they are sold like works of art and most likely change hands quietly between knowledgeable collectors.

★★★★ Almost the best. Prices are well into the five-figure range. These still come on the open market but all too rarely. There will always be a higher number of potential buyers for this model than the five star examples.

★★★ Excellent value. Desirable cars which have not attained a prohibitive asking price. Still good investment value over a longer period of time.

★★ Good cars to own and drive. Generally not considered exotic or having a ready resale market.

★ Any Maserati that has the wrong engine and is in need of total restoration. Not necessarily short of investment value, but rebuild costs can outstrip resale value.

The single most important point in purchasing a used Maserati is to find a model that, whatever its condition when you first see it, you find yourself envisioning only what it *should* be like. That "feeling" will propel you to put the Maserati in superb condition regardless of the time involved and, invariably, the amount of money it will absorb. Not always is it only the dollars that you require on top of the initial purchase price; in many, many instances it is the dedication and enthusiasm to right the wrongs of the car's previous life.

In 1970 I purchased four nonrunning 3500GT coupes for $1,500 total. When relating the story fifteen years later people say, "Oh, those days are surely gone." They forget that not only is it unlikely to happen to you now, but that the value of that $1,500 has risen with natural monetary deflation and economic inflation. Within reason, whatever the price of your Maserati today it will not depreciate fifteen years later, and you will have had in that time considerable enjoyment from it.

Following is a brief description of each Maserati built by the factory from 1947 to 1989. In a separate chapter, the competition cars are listed, since vintage racing is increasingly popular and there still remains the possibility of finding such a model, although not necessarily a complete one.

This car is a rare sight today, some thirty-seven years after its introduction as Maserati's first model for the consumer market, and with a total production of not more than sixty examples.

Shown to the public for the first time at the Geneva Salon in 1947, the gray A6-1500 was received with ample praise. The Pinin Farina design caused considerable excitement with its disappearing headlamps and Plexiglas sunroof. Such features are common on today's motor cars, but must have been unique in 1947.

The model was a two-door, two-seater coupe with upholstery in corduroy and rexin. Instrumentation consisted of speedometer reading in kph, water temperature gauge, oil pressure gauge and gas gauge, with the necessary knobs and switches of Bakelite. Naturally, an ashtray was included.

The engine design was a legacy from the Maserati brothers during their prewar era of building the 1500 cc six-cylinder voiturettes. Obviously, for a production unit, the supercharger and carburetor could not be incorporated, and the cylinder head underwent considerable rethinking. What emerged was an in-line six with chain-drive, single overhead camshaft, detachable cylinder head and single Weber carburetor. Installed in the robust A6 chassis, the engine was capable of moving the car at almost 90 mph, its 1½ liters developing 65 bhp at 4700 rpm. The engine proved reliable and simple to maintain, and the car was accepted as being practical, everyday transportation—for those who could afford such a purchase.

The coachbuilder Pinin Farina was responsible for bodying the entire A6-1500 production of sixty cars between 1946 and 1950. However, it should be noted that there was one A6 with coupe body by Zagato. Factory archives do not record this fact but this equally rare coupe is now in the possession of an Italian Maserati enthusiast, so its existence can be verified.

Competition was never far away from Maserati; and maybe once an owner had a car with such a famous ancestry he was motivated into action that he would not have previously considered. It is known that during 1947 and 1948 the A6 did make one or two race appearances at the hands of private owners.

Customers for the A6 Maserati were mainly confined to Italy, although toward the end of the 1½-liter production run, a few examples were delivered to the USA and South America. While this model was

Photographed in Turin in February 1947, the A6-1500 Maserati bodied by Pinin Farina.

This three-quarter-rear view illustrates the tidy design of trunk lid and necessary fittings. The short rear overhang is highlighted by the novel rear window style.

being built, full trading links with other countries were not pursued, since the home market proved large enough for the factory's production capacity. It must be remembered that the car was introduced only one year after World War II, when circumstances were anything but conducive for car constructors.

This early series of Maseratis has, during the past few years, become recognized as a landmark in both Maserati and Italian coachbuilding history. While the acquisition of such cars is based upon their rare availability and location, they are today much appreciated in Italy where several examples survive in original condition.

It is important to keep in mind the rarity of the A6. This historically significant car is almost more of a museum piece than a driving car, especially considering that its design is more impressive than its performance. It's very difficult to find parts for the A6, particularly the body, thus the necessity of locating a complete car. A perfect example would cost about $20,000 more than a restorable car. Those who favor performace and are inclined toward spirited driving will find the 2000 cc Maseratis more attractive.

SERIAL NUMBERS
1946: 051 and 052
1947: 053 to 055 inclusive
1948: 056 to 064 inclusive
1949 and 1950: 065 to 0110 inclusive

Engine
Type: . . . . A6-1500 (straight 6)
Bore x stroke, mm/inches: 66x72.5, 2.6x2.9
Displacement, cc: 1488
Valve operation: . . . . single overhead camshaft
Compression ratio: 7.8:1
Carburetion: . . . . .single 36DCR Weber
Bhp (factory): . . . . 65@4700 rpm
Chassis & Drivetrain
Clutch: . . . . single dry plate
Transmission: 4-speed
Rear suspension: . . . . coil spring,
hydraulic shock absorber
Front suspension: . . . . coil spring,
hydraulic shock absorber
Frame: . . . . tubular
General
Wheelbase, mm/inches: 2550, 102
Track, front, mm/inches: 1274, 50.9
rear, mm/inches: 1252, 50.1
Brakes: . . . . hydraulic, aluminum drum, iron liner
Tire size, front and rear: 5.50x16
Wheels: . . . . .pressed steel
Coachbuilder: . . . . .Pinin Farina

Another Pinin Farina design for the A6-1500 pictured in Milan on November 13, 1947.

The chassis of Maserati's 1½-liter six-cylinder car as it was delivered to the coachbuilder. Note the single carburetor with mushroom-type cover. The chassis is robust with rather agricultural coil springs.

As can be seen from this 1949 A6-1500, the original Pinin Farina design underwent several changes during its infancy.

The rear glass of the first model has disappeared, and the trunk lid has grown to the full depth of the tail. The A6 always looks better in a dark color with the fashionable chrome hubcaps, embossed with the Trident badge.

CHAPTER 2
A6G
1951-1953

Searching for more power from its road car engine, Maserati upgraded the single cam 1½-liter in 1951 to 2000 cc. Alterations to both bore and stroke, with improved breathing through triple Weber carburetors, resulted in the in-line six producing 35 bhp more than its predecessor. Dependent upon axle ratio and body constructer, this new model was capable of just 100 mph, which is what customers had asked for.

The first coachbuilder to construct on the A6G chassis was Pinin Farina with its almost regulation four-seater coupe; shown at the same time was a carbriolet from Frua. The latter was the first of three such models executed by Pietro Frua in 1951.

The domestic market was improving in Italy, and Omer Orsi considered 1951 an opportune time to offer this two-liter production model. The company was not wrong to produce such a car, but with its interests still greatly in motor racing, neither the engine nor chassis underwent any program of development. Handling was improved with the fitting of semi-elliptic leaf springs at the rear, but in all other respects the chassis was identical to the A6-1500.

During its production life, the A6G was bodied by only three coachbuilders; apart from the two already mentioned, Vignale created its coupe for the 1951 Paris Salon. This was a two-door, fastback design with a gorgeous profile, finished in yellow and blue, which caused a mild sensation. The car was affectionately singled out as being the two-liter with the "lira grin," owing to grille interpretation.

Sales of the A6G were handled almost exclusively by Guglielmo Dei, the Maserati dealer based in Rome. He did very well representing the marque and found customers in Italy, New York, Cuba and South America. Even so, total production and consequent sales did not exceed sixteen cars from 1951 to 1953.

The survival rate is not high, although the one-off Vignale coupe resides in California. An A6G is seldom seen on the open market, and in view of the few built this is not surprising.

In spite of the A6G's rarity and parts scarcity (more difficult to find parts for than even the A6), this model is beginning to attract serious collector interest in America. More cars are being restored—values fluctuate greatly depending on the body, especially for convertibles.

The pretty A6G cabriolet from Frua had a sporting appearance
although with a somewhat overstylized grille.

SERIAL NUMBERS
Pinin Farina coupes: 2013, 2020-2027 inclusive
Frua coupe: 2028
Frua cabriolets: 2015, 2017, 2018, 2029, 2030
Vignale coupe: 2031 (this number is shown in factory archives, but in
reality the surviving A6G by Vignale is stamped 2021)

Engine
Type:......................... A6G (straight 6)
Bore x stroke, mm/inches: 72x80, 2.9x3.2
Displacement, cc:............................1954
Valve operation:........ single overhead camshaft
Compression ratio: 7.8:1
Carburetion: ....triple 36 or 38 DO4 Weber
Bhp (factory): .... 100@5500 rpm
Chassis & Drivetrain
Clutch: .... single dry plate
Transmission: 4-speed
Rear suspension: .... leaf spring,
                      hydraulic shock absorber
Front suspension: .... coil spring
                      hydraulic shock absorber
Frame: .... tubular
General
Wheelbase, mm/inches: 2550, 102
Track, front, mm/inches:............... 1274, 50.9
        rear, mm/inches: 1252, 50.1
Brakes:....... hydraulic, aluminum drum, iron liner
Tire size, front and rear: 5.50x16
Wheels:............. pressed steel or Borrani wire
Coachbuilder: .... Pinin Farina, Pietro Frua,
                      Alfredo Vignale

The three-carburetor, two-liter single cam
Maserati engine introduced in 1951. A clean
design with cast aluminum cam cover always
finished in black.

The interior of the two-liter cabriolet illustrates its sporting pre-
tensions with riveted wood-rimmed steering wheel and rev counter. The white-faced clock in the dashboard (right) was a nice
touch.

From Pinin Farina came this rather austere A6G shown at Turin
in 1951.

Another Pinin Farina creation on the two-liter single cam chassis,
which was lower overall, with new grille treatment and overriders
fitted to the front bumper.

It is likely this was Frua's only design for a coupe on the A6G chassis. The car is pictured at the 1952 Turin show, and illustrates another design for the front which incorporates two spotlights. The car looks as though it would go faster than its single cam engine would permit.

CHAPTER 3
A6G/2000 (A6G/54)
1954-1957

The heritage of this new model, announced in 1954, lay with the sports A6GCS and not with the previous production car, the A6G. The factory had decided to make it on quite a large scale: a performance two-liter coupe powered by its twin cam engine. Maserati was obviously thinking of the competition appeal which the A6G did not embrace, and realized that a civilized version of the sports racing car could find an enthusiastic market. That thinking was not wrong, but it was successful mainly as a result of what Zagato created for this chassis. The new Maserati delivered all that was hoped for.

The engine of the A6G/2000 (A6GCS Series II) was reworked by engineer Luigi Bellentani to yield a reliable and tractable unit which could be simply tuned for additional performance if required. The noisy gear train was disposed of and a triple-row timing chain installed, driven via a series of sprockets from the crankshaft. The twin overhead camshafts operated large mushroom-shaped valves with individual screw adjusters. The dry-sump system was replaced with wet-sump lubrication, and a deep, finned sump in light alloy.

The first series of this engine had single-plug ignition with either thirty-six or thirty-eight D04 carburetors, later replaced with forty DC03 Webers and twelve spark plugs. Output was in excess of 150 hp at 6000 rpm, with lively acceleration and a top speed of over 115 mph.

As was normal with the factory, the management invited coachbuilders to design their own interpretations of the A6G/2000 Maserati. Zagato, Allemano and Frua offered customers a wide variety of body styles from which to choose.

The competition flavor was interpreted effectively by Zagato, which built some lovely coupe bodies which were light and functional. It also made a one-off spyder which was shown at the Geneva Salon in 1955. This slab-sided, boring convertible was not one of Zagato's better efforts, however.

Several Zagato-bodied two-liter Maseratis were used in GT racing throughout Italy from 1955 to 1957 and this model eventually won this class in the 1956 Italian championships which had previously been dominated by the powerful V-8 Fiats. This was a classic example of Maserati's ability to transfer the best qualities of its competition car into a production model; certainly a case of "racing improves the breed."

The series builder of coachwork on the A6G/2000 was Allemano, which offered a wide range of coupe styles, all well built with quality

The six-cylinder, twin cam two-liter Maserati engine with twin plug cylinder head and triple 40DC03 Weber carburetors.

One of the lovely A6G/2000 spyders from Frua with its regulation hood stripe.

interior fittings. Always cataloged as a Berlina, the Allemano design was a sober-looking car aimed at a more sedate type of Maserati buyer.

The coupes and spyders from Frua were similar to his earlier creations on the A6G. Frua spyders were lovely designs, invariably finished in two colors with a significant hood stripe, always looking fast and sporty.

On the road, the twin cam Maserati performed well, averaging 18 mpg (Imperial) driven hard. The chassis was "twitchy" in the wet, but with the light and precise steering, maneuvers were easily controlled. In dry conditions the roadholding was excellent; and once the gear changes were mastered, the car's character and manners brought out the best from the driver. Of course, there was a difference between a Zagato version and an Allemano or Frua. The former could be driven in a manner befitting its style and lighter weight, while no such undertaking would be attempted with the convertible or Allemano model.

Production of this popular Maserati ceased with chassis number 2198 in 1957, after fifty-nine examples had been built. It is possible to purchase one of these cars today, but there is a wide price difference between a Zagato coupe, an Allemano coupe and a Frua spyder. The model's survival rate is high, probably because many people know what a good engine and chassis the A6G/2000 possessed.

Of all Maserati road cars the A6G/2000 ranks with the Ghibli and Bora as the most desirable among enthusiasts. Although all are pricey, actual values vary widely due to the large production of one-offs. Zagato bodies rate the highest; next are the later Frua cars. You can expect to **pay from $200,000 to $400,000 for a complete, restorable car, depending on the bodywork—body pieces are impossible to find. But the excellent driving characteristics of this two-liter Maserati make finding and restoring one worthwhile.**

SERIAL NUMBERS
(Listed in the order they left the factory)
Zagato spyder: 2101
Zagato coupes: 2102, 2105, 2106, 2107, 2112, 2113, 2118, 2121, 2122, 2123, 2124, 2137, 2138, 2148, 2150, 2155, 2160, 2179, 2186, 2189
Allemano coupes: 2108, 2111, 2116, 2117, 2119, 2120, 2125, 2142, 2115, 2126, 2144, 2165, 2175, 2146, 2170, 2184, 2185, 2188, 2190, 2195, 2198
Frua coupes and spyders: 2103, 2109, 2114, 2140, 2180, 2187, 2181, 2182, 2183, 2197, 2191, 2193, 2192, 2194, 2196, 2104, 2110

Still retained by the Maserati factory today, an Allemano coupe
that illustrates a more refined interpretation of the two-liter car.

Fairly spartan interior of one of Zagato's coupes; the speedometer shows a maximum readout of 240 kph, which is somewhat optimistic.

It is possible that the original customer requested the top stripe and noseband on this shiny Zagato coupe.

This picture of a 1956 A6G/2000 Maserati illustrates well the low build of the Zagato models. All were slightly different in external features. The central rib ending at the hood badge is not offensive.

Engine
Type:............... A6G-2000 (A6G/54) (straight 6)
Bore x stroke, mm/inches: 76.5x72, 3.1x2.9
Displacement, cc:.............................1985
Valve operation:..........twin overhead camshaft
Compression ratio: 8:1
Carburetion: .... triple 36D04 or 38D04
or 40DC03 Weber
Bhp (factory): .... 160@6000 rpm
Chassis & Drivetrain
Clutch: .... single dry plate
Transmission: 4-speed
Rear suspension: .... quarter elliptic,
hydraulic shock absorber
Front suspension: .... coil spring,
hydraulic shock absorber
Frame: .... tubular
General
Wheelbase, mm/inches: 2250, 102
Track, front, mm/inches:............... 1360, 54.4
rear, mm/inches: 1220, 48.8
Brakes:....... hydraulic, aluminum drum, iron liner
Tire size, front and rear: 6.00x16
Wheels:........ Borrani wire, center-lock, knock-off
Coachbuilder: .... Zagato, Allemano, Frua

CHAPTER 4
3500GT
1957-1964

Marketed from 1957 to 1964 the 3500GT coupe was Maserati's financial salvation during a particularly difficult period. Motor racing expenses were high, even after the 1957 World Championship, and unpaid invoices to South America aggravated the losses. With the introduction of this consumer model, the management at long last placed Maserati among Italy's serious car manufacturers instead of competing in a half-hearted manner.

The prototype coupe, bodied by Touring of Milan with super-leggera (extra-light) construction, was shown at Geneva on March 20, 1957, and immediately underwent development in all areas (its styling was heavily influenced by the Ford Thunderbird). Within months, engineer Giulio Alfieri had redesigned the lubrication system, modified the camshafts and porting and gained another 4 bhp to yield a reliable 230 bhp at 5500 rpm. By the time of the Turin Salon later in 1957, the 3500GT was in regular, although still low-key, production and orders were coming in.

This coupe certainly had muscle and, although the early four-speed transmission was not totally favorable, the car could move quickly, with good handling characteristics giving a smooth ride for the occupants. The early four-wheel drum brakes, although servo assisted, were not effective enough in a hasty moment; under normal touring conditions, though, they could retard the aluminum coupe safely. The six-cylinder engine was, if anything, understressed, and made a truly glorious noise when accelerating hard.

Besides Touring of Milan coachwork, Allemano attempted four coupes in 1958-59, which, although extremely pretty, did not appeal to the management. Carrozzeria Bertone designed a 3500 coupe in 1959, and Pietro Frua styled a one-off spyder the same year; otherwise, total production coupes were constructed by Touring.

Front disc brakes were an option in late 1959, but on 1960 models were standard. One year later, the five-speed gearbox was introduced. And in 1962, the 3½-liter engine was fitted with fuel injection, giving improved economy yet more power.

The factory production line built seven 3500 coupes a week during 1960, plus eighty-eight of the shorter-wheelbase chassis on which Vignale mounted its steel-bodied covertible. The spyder from Vignale was well received on the home market and in the USA, where sales were handled by Maserati Corporation of America and, later, Bob Grossman.

A 1958 3500GT with Touring of Milan coachwork. The wire wheels were an expensive option offered by the factory.

A 1959 version with single quarter light successfully interrupting the wide door glass. The amber "torpedo" indicators were now on the side of each fender.

Its price in 1961, once in the USA, was $12,300; but owing to its relatively low production was not available off the showroom floor. Total production of this 3500 spyder was less than 250 in both left- and right-hand-drive form, from 1959 to 1964. Almost two thousand of the coupes were completed by Touring of Milan, with sales to virtually every country in the Western world. By 1962 its replacement was shown at Geneva, and Maserati was into its stride, operating a true production line.

Today, the 3500 series of Maserati coupes and convertibles retain a following by owners and enthusiasts which goes beyond mere loyalty. These cars represent quality motoring with a pedigree that few other manufacturers can match. They are satisfying to own and drive, and twenty years past their production their style is still exciting.

This first true production car to come from Maserati was highlighted by a quick (0-60 mph in 7.5 seconds, 0-100 in twenty seconds), high-torque engine that makes the 3500GT both exciting and easy to drive. It was also remarkable for its excellent quality of construction and materials (especially the coupes). The early cars are considered prettier with more handbuilt, low-volume features and details. Generally speaking, the 3500GT is a fine combination of timeless styling coupled with parts and service availability (though body parts are still on the difficult side). And the coupe alloy bodies eliminate rust worries—be sure to check the frame, however. The spyders are considered more rare and desirable but their steel bodies are a source of concern for rust.

Keep in mind that the early cars had the four-speed with drum brakes and carburetors; the last cars had discs, the five-speed and fuel injection. Be sure to check the oil pressure on fuel-injected cars. Many 3500GT's in America are being converted to carbs.

This is a good car for the beginning Maserati restorer since there are a number of restorable 3500's around at reasonable prices (about $20,000).

Engine
Type: ....3500GT (straight 6)
Bore x stroke, mm/inches: 86x100, 3.4x4
Displacement, cc: 3485
Valve operation: ....twin overhead camshaft
Compression ratio: 8.5:1
Carburetion: ....triple 42DCOE or fuel injection
Bhp (factory): .... 220@5500 rpm.
                                235@5800 rpm (injection)

Chassis & Drivetrain
Clutch: .... single dry plate
Transmission: .... 4- or 5-speed
Rear suspension: .... leaf spring,
                          hydraulic shock absorber

Front suspension: .... coil spring,
                          hydraulic shock absorber
Frame: .... tubular
General
Wheelbase, mm/inches: .... 2600, 102 (coupe);
                                2500, 100 (spyder)
Track, front, mm/inches:................ 1390, 55.6
        rear, mm/inches: 1360, 54.4
Brakes:.... aluminum drum, iron liner; disc, 1960 on
Tire size, front and rear: 6.50x16
Wheels:..........Borrani disc. or wire center-lock,
                                        knock-off
Coachbuilder: .. Allemano, Touring of Milan, Vignale

The first-series 3½-liter Maserati engine's affinity to the design of the 350S competition engine can be clearly seen.

From 1962 on the 3500 engine had direct Lucas fuel injection. Power output was increased and a smaller-diameter crankshaft fitted.

The definitive version of the 3500 series coupe, a 1962 model with fuel injection, five-speed gearbox and disc brakes.

An unsuccessful attempt by Touring of Milan to create a Maserati drophead. It is thought only five such examples were completed.

The 3500 Maserati convertible from Vignale was an instant success. From any angle this beautifully proportioned spyder was handsome to behold.

Interior of 1962 3500GT.

Top stowage was neat, and the trunk more than adequate for luggage for two. This is a 1963 version of the 3500GTI Maserati spyder.

CHAPTER 5
SEBRING
1962-1966

Although 1962 was a prolific year for 3500GT production Maserati decided to offer another 2+2 coupe that interpreted current automobile trends in this up-scale market. Created by Alfredo Vignale and constructed on the same short wheelbase chassis as his spyder, the 3500-GTIS (Sebring) was a steel-bodied, spacious two-seater with two smaller seats in the rear. On view at Geneva in early 1962, the design was as angular as the 3500 was curved. In outward appearance, and alongside Touring of Milan's coupe, the Sebring looked severe and more upright, lacking some of the gracefulness of the 3500GT.

The engine was basically the same reliable, in-line six but with longer stroke, and a revised block that incorporated two engine mounts instead of four. Fuel injection was incorporated, as it had been proved this increased torque and performance. In testing, the Sebring could achieve 135 mph and accomplish the standing quarter-mile in sixteen seconds. All Sebrings were fitted with five-speed ZF transmissions, but not all were 3700 cc. The first examples of this new model were powered by the current 3½-liter engine, and toward the end of its short production life the capacity was increased to 4000 cc.

Optional equipment was indeed plentiful; the factory showing a considerably fresh outlook. Automatic transmission, wire wheels, air conditioning, tinted glass, special paint, radio—the dealers could certainly make the most of adorning the Sebring.

Production of the first series totaled 348 from 1962 to 1965. Vignale then revised the model and built ninety-eight Series II cars in 1965 and 1966.

Not a great number of Sebrings were originally sold to buyers in the USA; the home market plus France and Switzerland yielded a good supply of customers. Right-hand-drive versions were sold into the UK and Australia; the latter, where the factory dealer was active, certainly purchased a high percentage.

It is interesting to note that after one year's production of the Sebring, the Maserati management contemplated offering another more sporting model, and maybe this speculation ruined the Sebring's market potential. This four-headlamp coupe was certainly not to everyone's liking and, in later times, the steel body influenced potential buyers against the model. But it was an essential progression for the factory, following the 3500 coupe with what was thought would be another volume seller.

Vignale's design for a 2+2 coupe on the shortened 3500GT chassis resulted in the Sebring; this is a Series I model with optional wire wheels.

Mechanically this Maserati is superb, and when driven fast reveals the better characteristics of its chassis, for the roadholding is very good as is the ride and comfort.

Very few excellent Sebring examples exist in America; prices run about the same as for the 3500GT—although the two cars appeal to different personalities. The Sebring is flashier and sportier whereas the 3500GT is more solid, classier and higher quality. The Sebring's small size and short wheelbase make for nimble handling.

Body parts for the rare Sebring are the most difficult to find of all Maserati production cars. It's especially important to locate a complete car if you have restoration in mind. The fuel injection can be rebuilt; many are replaced with Webers.

Engine
Type: . . . . Sebring (straight 6)
Bore x stroke, mm/inches: 86x106, 3.4x4.2
Displacement, cc: 3694
Valve operation: . . . . .twin overhead camshaft
Compression ratio: 8.8:1
Carburetion: . . . . .Lucas fuel injection
Bhp (factory): . . . . 245@5200 rpm
Chassis & Drivetrain
Clutch: . . . . single dry plate
Transmission: 5-speed
Rear suspension: . . . . semi-elliptic,
                                    hydraulic shock absorber
Front suspension: . . . . coil spring,
                                    hydraulic shock absorber
Frame: . . . . tubular
General
Wheelbase, mm/inches: 2500, 100
Track, front, mm/inches: 1390, 55.6
        rear, mm/inches: 1360, 54.4
Brakes: . . . . .disc
Tire size, front and rear: 185x16
Wheels: . Borrani disc. or wire center-lock, knock-off
Coachbuilder: . . . . Vignale
Note: The Sebring was fitted with either 3500, 3700 or
        4000 cc engine.

Interior with all essential dials directly in front of the driver. The row of three rocker switches seen on the left-hand side were only on the Series I models.

Frontal appearance was attractive and the grille style was certainly neat and tidy—more modern than the 3500GT.

The Sebring Series II introduced by Maserati in 1965. The car looks like a fast touring coupe—and it was.

Considerably improved interior with anodized-rim gauges, central console for switches and accessories, and the air-conditioning equipment above.

The Series II with revised headlamp and side lamp treatment, also the hood intake scoop is less obtrusive.

Mistral Coupe ★★★
Mistral Spyder ★★★★

Offered by Maserati as a more sporting alternative in 1964, the Mistral coupe designed by Pietro Frua was a complete break in style from the previous two models. From its initial showing at Turin in 1964 it was obvious this new car was going to be a popular replacement for the Sebring.

Seating had been reduced to just driver and passenger, with the space behind given over for luggage and, possibly, a small child. The hatchback rear-opening glass was a novel feature and dispensed with the extended trunk lid, enabling the designer to "blunt" the tail.

The first examples had the 3½-liter engine, but after 1964 the 3.7-liter unit was used exclusively. During 1966 a 4000 cc displacement engine was offered—the ultimate version of the six-cylinder Maserati production engine. In fact, on a power-to-weight basis the 4000 Mistral is the hottest production, road-going Maserati ever!

The Mistral was some 154 pounds (70 kgs) lighter than the Sebring, mainly achieved by a greater use of aluminum in the construction of doors and hood. Some coupes were all aluminum, but there was no apparent reason for this and, consequently, their total number is unknown.

The drophead version of the Mistral, with the 3½-liter engine, was shown at the Geneva Salon in 1964. This prototype created a warm response from both enthusiasts and potential buyers. Although the spyder never really got into its stride with volume production, 120 examples were completed between 1964 and the end of 1969. One spyder was built in 1970 with a four-liter engine, but this was the swan song of the six-cylinder as a production model. A Mistral spyder in 1968 cost $15,000 landed in America. Its competition in the high-priced sports car market was Ferrari, which gave the Maserati importer a tough time.

The Mistral coupe sold well in Europe and America. Just over 800 examples were completed by early 1970. Its looks and sporting appeal ensured the model's future, and today it has a high appreciation among lovers of Italian cars.

The Mistral marked the end of the era of the six-cylinder-powered production models, a period which stretched from 1958 to 1970, for the factory had long since decided to build cars with even greater performance and bigger engines.

With the same basic drive train as the 3500GT and Sebring, but featuring a more modern shape and more creature comforts, the Mistral ranks as more of a grand touring automobile than a sports car. Some

A 1966 version of Maserati's Mistral with wedge-shaped hood and air-intake grille located well beneath the bumper.

feel the hatchback (one of the very first; historically significant) shape is a bit heavy, but everyone loves convertibles. The spyder's beauty and extreme rarity make it a truly coveted vehicle.

Mistral engine parts are easy to get. Be sure to check the fuel-injection system carefully if it hasn't been rebuilt or replaced.

Engine
Type: . . . . .Mistral (straight 6)
Bore x stroke, mm/inches: 88x110, 3.4x4.3
Displacement, cc: 4014
Valve operation: . . . . .twin overhead camshaft
Compression ratio: 8.8:1
Carburetion: . . . . .Lucas fuel injection
Bhp (factory): . . . . 255@5500 rpm
Chassis & Drivetrain
Clutch: . . . . single dry plate
Transmission: 5-speed
Rear suspension: . . . . semi-elliptic,
            hydraulic shock absorber
Front suspension: . . . . coil spring,
            hydraulic shock absorber
Frame: . . . . tubular
General
Wheelbase, mm/inches: 2400, 96
Track, front, mm/inches: 1390, 55.6
        rear, mm/inches: 1360, 54.4
Brakes: . . . . .disc
Tire size, front and rear: 205x15
Wheels: . . . . Borrani wire, center-lock, knock-off
Coachbuilder: . . . . Frua
Note: The Mistral was fitted with either 3500, 3700 or 4000 cc engine.

The interior was comfortable, with a fully adjustable seat and steering column, offering a wide range of driving positions. Some gear knobs were wood, others black plastic; all controls were easily reached.

The spyder Mistral was a very handsome motor car, and today is a highly coveted Maserati.

The novelty which especially appealed to the American buyer
was that the entire rear window swung upward on two substantial
hinges hidden within the roof line.

Installation of the in-line six-cylinder in the Mistral. Beneath the fuel metering unit is a large, plastic air-intake box.

Not many convertible owners took advantage of purchasing the optional hardtop; the two flying buttresses did not enhance the Mistral's good looks.

CHAPTER 7
5000GT
1960-1964

The five-liter road car built by Maserati in small numbers between 1960 and 1964 was a fairly audacious exercise for any motor manufacturer. Many well-known and influential persons were faithful customers of the factory, and when looking at the list of original buyers of this model, it can be appreciated why this extravagant Maserati was built.

The power unit chosen for this exclusive machine was the V-8 sports racing engine, used to good effect in the 450S of 1957. In fact, apart from some mild detuning, the initial three 5000GT road cars used exactly that engine. Later, the four gear-driven overhead camshafts were altered to chain drive, and in some instances the vertical Weber carburetors were replaced with Lucas fuel injection. To absorb the 350 bhp, engineer Alfieri made appropriate alterations to the tubular 3500 chassis, incorporating disc brakes on the front wheels only.

The first showing of this ultimate road-going toy was at the Turin exhibition in 1959, where Touring of Milan displayed its Shah creation. This same coachbuilder completed numbers 1, 2 and 3 of the 5000GT along similar lines.

Following this initial showing there came a steady number of inquiries for the 5000GT from all parts of the world. The factory only cataloged the Allemano version, since the remainder was created by several Italian coachbuilders to their customers' specific instruction.

The Ghia-bodied five-liter which was commissioned by Sig. Innocenti was road tested by Bernard Cahier in 1961. The test results, printed in *Sports Car Graphic* in 1962, indicated the car was capable of 152 mph. A previous article, written by Hans Tanner and reprinted in a European motoring journal, had recorded a terminal speed in excess of 170 mph. Whichever version is correct, the 5000GT was undeniably a very quick road car.

At a price of almost twice the 3500GT coupe, the factory's distributors only ordered the model after receiving a substantial deposit. Customers such as the Shah of Persia, Briggs Cunningham, Sig. Agnelli (of Fiat) and Aga Khan were among the small nucleus of rich connoisseurs who owned one of these Maseratis.

In true Maserati style they were of individual construction and sold exclusively in a market which could absorb such characteristics. In this respect the 5000GT was a success and prompted Maserati to introduce the Quattroporte, a luxury model of more civilized proportions and realistic cost.

The mean-looking 5000GT Maserati. This is one of the twenty examples built by Allemano, which was the series coachbuilder on this chassis.

Practically all of the thirty-two examples that were made survive today, although somewhat scattered geographically. They never were considered everyday motor cars when new and, possibly for that reason, they mostly remain in original, full working condition.

Ambitious would be one way of summing up Maserati's aims with the 5000. Rare and expensive goes without saying. This ultimate car is reminiscent of Duesenbergs in the thirties or the Aston Martin Lagonda of more modern times. Most examples contain a number of unique features. Of the thirty-two built, approximately twenty were done by Allemano.

The combination of brutal acceleration, primitive handling and luxury-car plushness makes for an exciting automobile indeed. Should you happen to acquire one of these rarities be sure you get a complete car; there are no body pieces left at all.

Engine
Type: 5000GT (V-8)
Bore x stroke, mm/inches: 98.5x81, 3.9x3.2
Displacement, cc: 4935
Valve operation: . . . . four overhead camshafts
Compression ratio: 8.5:1
Carburetion: . . . . four 45 or 46IDM Webers or
fuel injection
Bhp (factory): . . . . 340/350@6000 rpm
Chassis & Drivetrain
Clutch: . . . . twin dry plate
Transmission: . . . . .4- or 5-speed
Rear suspension: . . . . semi-elliptic,
hydraulic shock absorber
Front suspension: . . . . coil spring,
hydraulic shock absorber
Frame: . . . . tubular
General
Wheelbase, mm/inches: 2600, 104
Track, front, mm/inches: 1390, 55.6
rear, mm/inches: 1360, 54.4
Brakes: . . . . .disc and drum rear or disc all round
Tire size, front and rear: 6.50x16
Wheels: . . . . Borrani disc or wire
Coachbuilder: . . . . Touring of Milan, Allemano, Pinin
Farina, Ghia, Frua, Bertone, Monterosa

Interior of serial number 056, a 1963 Allemano version of the five-liter. The two large dials—rev counter and speedometer—house within themselves the oil temperature and pressure gauges, and fuel tank capacity and water temperature gauges. The three-spoke steering wheel allowed adequate visibility of the gauges.

Carrozzeria Ghia created this very luxurious 5000GT in 1961. The car has a very low overall height accentuated by the creative wheel arches.

Stylized nose treatment on the Shah of Persia's
1959 5000GT from Touring of Milan.

The Michelotti-designed 5000GT, serial number 016 consigned
to that great motoring enthusiast, Briggs Cunningham, in 1962.

This photograph of the Ghia version shows sunroof and unusual metal sculpture for the front bumper. The car was built on chassis 018 for Sig. Innocenti.

Quattroporte 1963-69 ★★
Quattroporte II 1974-77 ★★★
Quattroporte 1979- ★★

QUATTROPORTE 1963-1969

This chapter covers three different designs, all with the same model name. To eliminate any confusion, three specification tables are given. The important points with regard to this Maserati are as follows:

The Quattroporte was introduced at the Turin motor show in 1963, with four-door coachwork by Frua. It had a 4.2-liter, V-8 engine and de Dion rear axle. The idea behind its manufacture was to offer a more practical version of the 5000GT, a model which had made the Maserati management aware of a consumer market for a high-powered sedan (saloon).

The Quattroporte was upgraded and shown in revised form in November 1965. The revisions included interior refinements, headlamps changed from rectangular to twin circular, live rear axle and 4.7-liter engine. The factory offered this version from 1966 on. The car was phased out of production at the end of 1969 after 759 examples had been completed.

Make no mistake, this was a large automobile; a fast, comfortable tourer comparable to the Mercedes 600. Although its styling was questionable it was a good car for the money. The interiors were very plush. In today's market these sedans don't attract the same attention as the sports models—they also tend to be less abused—so prices are relatively low. You should have no problem getting parts for the V-8 engine.

QUATTROPORTE II 1974-1977

Introduced at the Turin motor show in November 1974, the Quattroporte II had four-door coachwork by Carrozzeria Bertone and a three-liter, V-6 engine. The production of this model suffered from industrial strikes and a disastrous marriage between Citroën and Maserati. Many considered the car nothing more than a Citroën SM; in this respect it may be fortuitous that the Quattroporte II never went into series production, which had been scheduled for January 1975.

It is known that five examples were completed. The prototype 002 was retained by the factory; 004 and 006 were 1976 cars; 008 and 010 were built in 1977. One was sold into Spain, one to South America and two or more to Saudi Arabia.

The Quattroporte II is so rare that many Maserati enthusiasts have never even seen one of these cars. It is essentially a prototype and

The V-8 engine installed in the Quattroporte of 1964. Although the two cylinder heads were cast for twin plugs, only single ignition was employed. The substantial black plastic cover houses the air filter.

The Maserati "sedan" introduced in 1963 offered comfort for five people in a manner less opulent than the 5000GT.

may be a good investment, but don't plan to drive it regularly. There is also a suspicion that this largish car might be on the slow side.

QUATTROPORTE 1979-

It was announced in 1976 by Maserati that a V-8 version of the Quattroporte II would be available, called Quattroporte. This was scheduled for 1978, but did not happen until 1979. The car was outwardly totally different than the V-6 version, and was exhibited at the Geneva Salon in early 1979. Apart from detailed refinements, the current Maserati Quattroporte is powered by their standard V-8 engine, while the chassis/body unit is constructed in the Biturbo factory, and not at Bertone.

The main feature of this Quattroporte is the beatiful interior of the car. In many ways it is comparable to the Mercedes 450SE.

After 1985 the Quattroporte was available only with the 4.9 liter engine, but in all other respects the design remained unchanged since 1976.

In 1987 the model name was replaced with Royale, and the engine was modified to give 280 hp with compression increased to 9.5:1. Speed was improved, the factory quoting 150 mph with the manual version.

Engine
Type: . . . . Quattroporte (V-8)
Bore x stroke, mm/inches: 88x85, 3.5x3.4
Displacement, cc: 4136
Valve operation: . . . . four overhead camshafts
Compression ratio: 8.5:1
Carburetion: . . . . four 38DCLN5 Webers
Bhp (factory): . . . . 260@5000 rpm
Chassis & Drivetrain
Clutch: . . . . single dry plate
Transmission: 5-speed
Rear suspension: . . . .de Dion (pre-1966), leaf spring, hydraulic shock absorber
Front suspension: . . . . coil spring, hydraulic shock absorber
Frame: . . . . .integral chassis/body unit
General
Wheelbase, mm/inches: 2750, 110
Track, front, mm/inches: 1390, 55.6
          rear, mm/inches: 1400, 56
Brakes: . . . . .disc
Tire size, front and rear: 205x15
Wheels: . . . . .Borrani disc
Coachbuilder: . . . . Frua
Note: After 1965 the engine was 4700 cc (bore x stroke 94x85 mm, 3.76x3.4 inches). Optional 4200 cc available until 1967.

Engine
Type: . . . . .Quattroporte II (V-6)
Bore x stroke, mm/inches: 91.6x75, 3.6x3
Displacement, cc: 2965
Valve operation: . . . . four overhead camshafts
Compression ratio: 8.8:1
Carburetion: . . . . triple 44DCNF Weber
Bhp (factory): . . . . 210@6000 rpm
Chassis & Drivetrain
Clutch: . . . . single dry plate
Transmission: 5-speed
Rear suspension: . . . . hydro-pneumatic
Front suspension: . . . . hydro-pneumatic
Frame: . . . . .integral chassis/body unit
General
Wheelbase, mm/inches: 3070, 122.8
Track, front, mm/inches: 1520, 60.8
          rear, mm/inches: 1490, 59.6
Brakes: . . . . .disc
Tire size, front and rear: . . . . 205/70 VR 15
Wheels: . . . . disc
Coachbuilder: . . . . .Bertone

Revised headlamp treatment identifies the upgraded Quattroporte, built commencing in 1965. This is the 4700 cc version with
live rear axle.

Instruments of the 4.7 Quattroporte were identical to those in
the Maserati Sebring, but rocker switches and heater location
were changed.

The 1979 Maserati Quattroporte with considerably redesigned coachwork by Bertone.

Here's a 1987 or 1988 Royale four-door. Apart from the name change little else appears to have been altered externally. Under the hood there's another 20 hp. The last big sedan called Royale was a Bugatti!

Expensive leather with walnut veneers were used in the Quattroporte interior. This current production model is aimed at an exclusive market.

Engine
Type: .... Quattroporte (V-8)
Bore x stroke, mm/inches: 88x85, 3.5x3.4
Displacement, cc: 4135
Valve operation: .... four overhead camshafts
Compression ratio: 8.5:1
Carburetion: .... four 42DCNF6 Webers
Bhp (factory): .... 255@6000 rpm
Chassis & Drivetrain
Clutch: .... single dry plate
Transmission: .... 5-speed or automatic
Rear suspension: .... coil spring,
hydraulic shock absorber
Front suspension: .... coil spring,
hydraulic shock absorber
Frame: ....integral chassis/body unit
General
Wheelbase, mm/inches: 2800, 112
Track, front, mm/inches: 1525, 61
rear, mm/inches: 1525, 61
Brakes: .... ventilated disc
Tire size, front and rear: 225/70 VR15
Wheels: .... light alloy disc
Coachbuilder: .... Bertone, Maserati factory
Note: Optional engine capacity of 4900 cc, bore x
stroke 93.9x89 mm, 3.7x3.5 inches, developing
280 bhp @ 5600 rpm. All US cars were 4.9.

The current V-8 Quattroporte. Even for its size this Maserati is an extremely elegant motor car.

CHAPTER 9
MEXICO
1965-1968

As a compliment to the Quattroporte, another performance Grand Tourer was shown in prototype form by Maserati in late 1965. Its name, Mexico, was given in recognition of the Formula One Cooper Maserati's win in that country's Grand Prix.

This new two-door coupe had an overall height twelve inches lower than the Quattroporte, yet could easily accommodate four people in comfort, with ample luggage capacity. Originally powered by the 4700 cc version of Maserati's smooth V-8 engine, it was later offered with the less-thirsty 4.2-liter version. Top speed of the car was 135 mph, although acceleration was not impressive, since the Mexico weighed (dry) around 3,400 pounds. The car was capable of high-speed cruising and its chassis had no known vices.

Customers for this Maserati were mostly from Europe, although America also accepted this luxurious car, even with its conservative style. Automatic gearbox, air conditioning and power steering were optional extras, the latter rather necessary since the car was a heavy-weight.

Total production of the Mexico did not number more than 250, all left-hand-drive, and was dropped from the ranks at the end of 1968. However, it did appear on the factory show stands in Paris and Geneva in 1969, 1970 and 1971.

Like the 3500GT, the Mexico is a Maserati with excellent, time-less styling. Highlights of this model are its comfortable ride and luxurious interior. The coupe body style has resulted in the Mexico being less abused than Maserati sports cars; therefore, they tend to be in relatively better shape. Do be cautious of rust on any example you are considering. Parts for the V-8 engine are easy to obtain. Less easy is establishing values for the Mexico because of its rarity. By early 1984 an excellent example had sold in the US for more than $28,000; but in 1989 this price doubled, although it is a Maserati which does not have a high audience appeal.

The Maserati Mexico with coachwork by Vignale offered a more pleasing design than its predecessor, the four-door.

The steel-bodied 4700 Mexico with rubber inserts in the overriders. The trunk lid was opened by a lever inside the car.

Typically Maserati: a well made, softly furnished interior with all controls convenient. The wood-rimmed steering wheel was a sporting fixture on all Mexicos.

Engine
Type: .... Mexico (V-8)
Bore x stroke, mm/inches: 93.9x85, 3.7x3.4
Displacement, cc: 4719
Valve operation: .... four overhead camshafts
Compression ratio: 8.5:1
Carburetion: .... four 38DCNL5 Webers
Bhp (factory): .... 290@5500 rpm
Chassis & Drivetrain
Clutch: .... single dry plate
Transmission: .... 5-speed or automatic
Rear suspension: ....semi-elliptic leaf spring, hydraulic shock absorber

Front suspension: .... coil spring, hydraulic shock absorber
Frame: ....integral chassis/body unit
General
Wheelbase, mm/inches: 2640, 105.6
Track, front, mm/inches: 1390, 55.6
      rear, mm/inches: 1360, 54.4
Brakes: ....disc
Tire size, front and rear: 205x15
Wheels: .... Borrani wire, center-lock, knock-off
Coachbuilder: ....Vignale
Note: Also offered with the 4200 cc engine (bore x stroke 88x85 mm, 3.5x3.4 inches).

CHAPTER 10
GHIBLI
1967-1973

Ghibli Coupe ★★★★
Ghibli Spyder ★★★★★

Still relying on its excellent V-8 engine, which the factory could build in varying capacities of 4200 to 4900 cc, Maserati continued to market a wide variety of motor cars for the discerning public. Always offering a mixture of coupe, 2+2 and limousine, in 1966 Maserati placed on the market a definite sports machine that looked as though it could run the autostrada forever.

In September 1966, Omer Orsi was in the Ghia design studio in Turin inspecting a life-size model of the new car from a design by the brilliant Giorgetto Giugiaro. This designer had been playing with his pencil sketches since 1965 to create a very low, aggressive-looking coupe for Maserati. The design was totally accepted by potential customers, who had to wait until 1967 before the Ghibli went into production at Modena.

The steel-bodied car was relatively heavy, but could achieve the standing quarter-mile in 17.7 seconds with an ultimate velocity of 160 mph. Criticisms were few, but a recurring observation was that at very high speed the front had a tendency to lift, lightening the steering and giving the driver a nervous moment. In spite of its low roof line, forty-six inches overall height, the Ghibli coupe was a spacious car and could accommodate some very tall owners—including basketball star Wilt Chamberlain.

In 1967 and 1968 total production of the Ghibli reached 373; and orders, especially from the USA, were continuing at a healthy rate. In 1969 the convertible interpretation of this coupe was announced, and immediately it was obvious the factory had another winner. This was indeed a delicious drophead symbolizing the very essence of a Maserati and illustrating the Italian coachbuilder's art at its finest.

Only 125 Ghibli spyders were built from 1969 to 1972, inclusive. Of this number, fewer than six were right-hand drive and possibly no more than twenty-five were SS versions, which was a convertible with the 4.9 engine. The last year of the spyder was 1972. The coupe continued in production one more year, by which time 1,149 examples had been sold. In truth, the demise of the Ghibli was hastened only by the mid-engine fashion which, for the factory, started in 1971. In the meantime, Maserati offered what it considered to be a four-seater version of the Ghibli, this time from Vignale, which became available in 1969.

The Ghibli has been referred to as the most beautiful sports/GT of all time. Its live rear axle, however, provides a "traditional" ride that

Dramatic lines of the Maserati Ghibli designed by Giorgetto Giugiaro while at Carrozzeria Ghia in 1966.

For the American market in 1970, the Ghibli coupe acquired the essential side indicators front and back. Fortunately however, they did little to ruin the style.

seems somewhat out of character with the modern styling. The stiffly sprung car does corner excellently though. You'll find the steering heavy at low speeds, but then no Maserati was really meant to be driven slowly.

The exterior styling of the Ghibli is matched by equally gorgeous interiors. Ghibli spyders are the most sought after GT Maseratis; their rarity and desirability have resulted in prices about triple what a comparable 3500GT would sell for. A good Ghibli tucked away in your garage would be an exceptional investment. The spyder's detachable hardtop would be a very rare find.

Although parts are available, do watch for rust on the front of the hood. And note also that the oil sump may need to be cleaned out; not doing so may cause oil pressure fluctuations.

A final way of describing this big, fast cruiser would be to say that the Ghibli is comparable to the Ferrari Daytona but at one quarter the price—at the moment! At the prestigious Monaco sale during May 1989, a lovely Ghibli spyder SS was sold for $300,000 and a similar-condition coupe for $105,000.

Engine
Type: ....Ghibli (V-8)
Bore x stroke, mm/inches: 93.9x85, 3.7x3.4
Displacement, cc: 4719
Valve operation: .... four overhead camshafts
Compression ratio: 8.5:1
Carburetion: .... four 42DCNF5 Webers
Bhp (factory): .... 330@5500 rpm

Chassis & Drivetrain
Clutch: .... single dry plate
Transmission: .... 5-speed or automatic
Rear suspension: ....semi-elliptic leaf spring, hydraulic shock absorber
Front suspension: .... coil spring, hydraulic shock absorber
Frame: .... tubular

General
Wheelbase, mm/inches: 2550, 102
Track, front, mm/inches: 1440, 57.6
    rear, mm/inches: 1420, 56.8
Brakes: .... disc
Tire size, front and rear: 215x15
Wheels: ...... Borrani wire, or light magnesium disc
Coachbuilder: ....Ghia
Note: Introduced in 1970 with the 4900 cc V-8 engine (bore x stroke 93.9x89 mm, 3.7x3.5 inches) and designated Ghibli SS.

Vertical overriders with rubber inserts were also fitted to the front bumper; again for import into America.

Seen at the Turin show in 1970 was this Ghibli SS, the 4900 cc version. The spyder was fitted with bolt-on wire wheels with the American tidbits added.

Stunning! The 1969 Ghibli spyder was an instant success for Maserati and has remained a classic automobile ever since.

Interior of an SS spyder, showing the then-current design trend for rocker switches and unobtrusive instrument layout. The driver sat rather low down, and the fully adjustable steering column was slightly angled.

Also at the 1970 Turin show, Maserati displayed a European version of the Ghibli spyder. This was a 4.7-liter model.

In 1968, not only was Maserati building the straight-six-cylinder cars, but complementing them with a range of V-8-powered models like the Quattroporte, Mexico and Ghibli. However, the Quattroporte was due to be phased out, which would have left the factory bereft of a four-seater coupe. The design of a replacement for the Quattroporte and Mexico was essential if all tastes in the market were to be catered to by Maserati.

Toward the close of 1968, the Indy (with steel coachwork by Vignale) was exhibited, powered by the 4.2-liter version of the V-8. Its foremost quality was its generous accommodation which could seat four people, forward of the deeply enclosed luggage compartment. Visibility was good, although owing to a low seating position the extent of the hood could not fully be seen, an annoying aspect especially when parking this Maserati. The first models did not have power steering as standard equipment, which was a mistake, since the 3,520-pound (1,600 kg) coupe was no lightweight and in traffic was fairly tiring to maneuver.

Production commenced in 1969 but customers came in surprisingly low numbers. The following year, however, the factory sold almost 300 of these well-appointed coupes.

The Indy was certainly in the "image" of the Ghibli. Its design proved to have excellent aerodynamics, resulting in low wind noise and relatively economical fuel consumption at 15-17 mpg.

The model was revised in 1972 and offered with the 4700 engine. One year later this variation gave way to the 4.9-liter engine, which was then used in all Indys until production ceased. With adaptations to meet legislated requirements, the Indy America was also sold in the USA until the close of production in 1974.

The model achieved sales success around the world and 1,136 examples were produced. It was Maserati's best-selling four-seater, and second-best-selling production car after the Ghibli.

But the era for automobiles like the Indy was temporarily fading. The mid-engine two-seater fashion was influencing even for Maserati which admittedly enjoyed building large-capacity, front-engine coupes and GT's.

The Indy was a pleasant combination of Mexico-like function with more external design flair. And, of course, don't forget the ex-

Interior was well endowed with all the comforts and offered enough space for four adults, although entry for the rear passengers was awkward.

The Maserati Indy was a four-seater GT coupe, ideal for long-distance journeys.

tremely comfortable, luxurious interior. Power steering would be a very desirable option. Body pieces are difficult to get, and rust on the Indy may be a problem, so be careful. Engine and driveline parts are readily available. A nice Indy should run less than half of what you'd pay for a decent Ghibli, but rust-free low-mileage examples of this high-speed G.T. Maserati are proving difficult to locate and consequently only a general price guide is possible.

Engine
Type: . . . . Indy (V-8)
Bore x stroke, mm/inches: 88x85, 3.5x3.4
Displacement, cc: 4136
Valve operation: . . . . four overhead camshafts
Compression ratio: 8.5:1
Carburetion: . . . . four DCLN5 Webers
Bhp (factory): . . . . 260@5500 rpm
Chassis & Drivetrain
Clutch: . . . . single dry plate
Transmission: . . . . 5-speed or automatic
Rear suspension: . . . . semi-elliptic leaf spring,
 hydraulic shock absorber
Front suspension: . . . . coil spring,
 hydraulic shock absorber
Frame: . . . . integral chassis/body unit
General
Wheelbase, mm/inches: 2600, 104
Track, front, mm/inches: 1480, 59.2
 rear, mm/inches: 1434, 57.4
Brakes: . . . . disc
Tire size, front and rear: 205VRx14
Wheels: . . . . light alloy
Coachbuilder: . . . . Vignale
Note: Also available with 4700 and 4900 cc engines.

With all the flaps open the very wide doors and large rear glass panel (which closed rather too quickly) can be observed.

This photograph, taken at the Turin show in 1970, illustrates the designer's ability to make the Indy appear smaller than it actually was.

CHAPTER 12
KHAMSIN
1974-1981

The respected *Road & Track* magazine said of this new Maserati in 1975, "The Khamsin is an ego trip on wheels." First shown to the public in 1972 at the Turin show, and then at the 1973 Paris Salon, the Khamsin was not put on sale until 1974.

The steel-bodied GT was supposed to be a 2+2, but in reality the space behind the front seats lacked head and leg room for adults. The Bertone coachwork, designed by Marcello Gandini, was extremely elegant, although the vertical rear glass panel caused raised eyebrows among its critics. The twin headlamps were hydraulically operated and, when closed, accentuated the sharp nose design which ended in a narrow bumper surrounding the side lights.

The interior was well laid out and most comfortable, with the very wide doors affording easy access. Trunk space was adequate; the rear-opening glass was controlled from within the cockpit. The low seats were fully adjustable by the hydraulic system, and offered a wide range of positions.

On the road, the Khamsin achieved full marks for comfort and performance, achieving 0-100 mph in twenty seconds with a top speed of 140 mph. Not only was this Maserati faster and more agile than its counterparts (the Lamborghini Espada, V-8 Aston Martin and Jensen Interceptor), but it was lighter and more economical.

Criticisms were mostly aimed at the ultra-quick steering and responsive brakes, both hydraulically controlled by use of a Citroën patent. In fairness, you have to live with a Khamsin a little longer than just a test drive; but once the technique of steering the car with such a sensitive system is mastered, its maneuverability is superb. The brakes must be described as effective and perfectly safe, but are not designed for a heavy or insensitive foot.

The factory found a worldwide market for the Khamsin which was built in low volume from 1974 until 1981. It was then phased out of production in favor of the five-seater Quattroporte.

Few expensive motor cars increase in charisma; many buyers become bored and are not prepared to suffer with the niggling faults associated with exotic Italian automobiles. Apparently Khamsin owners are not so inclined, preferring to develop a lengthy relationship with this Maserati. Certainly it is one of the supercars, and maybe one of the last of its kind from Maserati. For sheer *looks* the Khamsin will always be appreciated.

Production of the Maserati Khamsin began in 1974; the crisp, yet elegant, coachwork is certainly Bertone. The intake grille on the nose was introduced on 1977 models.

When shopping for a Khamsin it is very important to remember the necessity of making sure the hydraulics are in good shape. Servicing the ultrasensitive steering and brakes can be a problem—having them work makes piloting this large, heavy car quite pleasant. One other problem area is the exhaust headers on the US versions; they can easily be converted to European headers.

Most would give the Khamsin excellent marks for styling—this is one of the very last front-engined, high-performance, exotic Italian GT's.

Engine
Type: .... Khamsin (V-8)
Bore x stroke, mm/inches: 93.9x89, 3.7x3.5
Displacement, cc: 4930
Valve operation: .... four overhead camshafts
Compression ratio: 8.5:1
Carburetion: .... four 42DCNF6 Webers
Bhp (factory): .... 320@5500 rpm
Chassis & Drivetrain
Clutch: .... single dry plate
Transmission: .... 5-speed or automatic
Rear suspension: .... coil spring,
                    hydraulic shock absorber
Front suspension: .... coil spring,
                    hydraulic shock absorber
Frame: ....integral chassis/body unit
General
Wheelbase, mm/inches: 2548, 100.3
Track, front, mm/inches:................1438, 56.6
        rear, mm/inches: 1465, 57.7
Brakes:.....................................disc
Tire size, front and rear: 215/70VRx15
Wheels:......................... light alloy disc
Coachbuilder: ....Bertone

The faithful and reliable 90° V-8 Maserati 4900 cc engine. The
small-bore pipework carried fluid for steering and brakes, a legacy
from the time when the Modena works was under Citroën ownership.

This picture of a 1975 Khamsin well illustrates the low seating
position and well-laid-out controls.

A Khamsin bodyshell being moved from paint shop to component assembly area within the factory. Taillight lenses were fitted below the rear glass on models exported to the USA.

Pictured within the factory compound in 1975 is a Khamsin about to run the autostrada as a test. The warning sign on the door indicates to other road users that the driver may stop suddenly and for no apparent reason.

It will always remain open to discussion as to whether the Kyalami is a Maserati or not. But since it carries the Trident badge on the hood and is powered by the Maserati V-8 engine, the car must be included in the product range.

The Kyalami was based on the De Tomaso Longchamp (a three-liter, two-door 2+2), introduced by De Tomaso in 1971-72. After De Tomaso acquired control of the Maserati factory, he commissioned Frua in Turin to revise the model. Alessandro De Tomaso named the Kyalami after the South African Grand Prix circuit, and exhibited this new creation at the Turin motor show in 1976.

It certainly was a thinly disguised Longchamp, but the iron V-8 engine had been replaced by the smooth, 4.2-liter Maserati unit, and the original chassis had undergone major revision. The design was not elegant, but smart, with clean, sharp lines, low overall height and more than a hint of muscle.

Detail modifications were carried out on the Kyalami, both to the coachwork and interior. Although delivery was scheduled for December 1976, it was not available until well into the following year. The model was not marketed in America, where strict car-import-control laws made life too difficult for low-volume constructors, but was sold in Europe and, in right-hand-drive versions, to UK customers.

The Kyalami was not a Maserati development of any kind. It merely proved that De Tomaso could integrate his two car factories into one manufacturing venture, which is what he had claimed when he took control at Modena.

The Kyalami should not be underrated as an Italian GT, for it offers quality and comfort with high performance and individual looks. But it was high-priced, expensive to run and not built in true Maserati fashion.

The 1976 Maserati Kyalami bodied by Carrozzeria Frua for De
Tomaso.

Engine
Type:................................. Kyalami (V-8)
Bore x stroke, mm/inches: 88x85, 3.5x3.4
Displacement, cc:.........................4136
Valve operation:.......... four overhead camshafts
Compression ratio: 8.5:1
Carburetion: .... four 42DCNF6 Webers
Bhp (factory): .... 265@6000 rpm
Chassis & Drivetrain
Clutch: .... single dry plate
Transmission: .... 5-speed or automatic
Rear suspension: .... coil spring,
hydraulic shock absorber

Front suspension: .... coil spring,
hydraulic shock absorber
Frame: ....integral chassis/body unit
General
Wheelbase, mm/inches: 2600, 104
Track, front, mm/inches:................ 1530, 61.2
rear, mm/inches: 1530, 61.2
Brakes:..............................disc
Tire size, front and rear: 205/70 VRx15
Wheels:.............light alloy or magnesium disc
Coachbuilder: .... Frua
Note: Offered with the 4900 cc engine in 1978.

CHAPTER 14
BORA
1971-1980

The Bora commission was given to Ital Design in 1969 with a brief for a V-8 mid-engine sports car with good ride, roadholding and aerodynamic looks. The design from Giorgetto Giugiaro resulted in the Maserati factory building the Bora in time for the 1971 Geneva Salon. This new Maserati was a break in both design and tradition from anything it had previously produced, although the 4.7-liter engine was now in its twelfth year of production.

This V-8 Maserati engine was a truly versatile power unit, and gave the Modena engineers few problems in either its assembly or maintenance. Maserati forgings, castings and machining were of the highest quality, and the factory mechanics could assemble the V-8 extremely quickly prior to dyno testing. The V-8's variations of cubic capacity, valve timing, carburetors and layout of ancillary equipment were all of totally proven design which, by its continual use, must have played an important commercial role in the development of each new model.

The Bora was another Maserati fitted with the controversial Citroën hydraulics; but the controversy over this technical feature was leveled by critics who really had limited experience with the system in a Maserati. Besides the brakes, the pedals fitted to the Bora were also hydraulically adjustable. This feature, together with the up-and-down adjustment of the seats and rake of the steering column, could give a wide range of driving positions. Some Boras did have conventional controls.

Rear vision through the large glass area was not very good. The Bora's heating and ventilating system was also poor.

But on the road, the car was superb—having no bad manners or vices—and the five-speed ZF gearbox was a delight to use once the warm oil had circulated. The Bora had a top speed of almost 175 mph, and could accelerate to 80 mph in ten seconds using only the first two gears. Noise level was very low and it was possible to hold an audible conversation with your passenger while moving along at 150 mph. The raucous racing noises invariably associated with mid-engine coupes of large displacement were not applicable to the Bora.

Between 1971 and the end of 1978 almost 500 examples had been sold; the model only hesitated in 1976 when it looked as though De Tomaso would close Bora production. This did not happen until 1980, by which time the Bora was powered by the 4900 cc engine, and total production had exceeded 550 cars.

Maserati's first production mid-engine car: the 1971 Bora 4700 cc.

The Bora from Maserati, like the Miura from Lamborghini, should never have ceased production, for it was a powerful, yet civilized, mid-engine coupe of balanced proportions which had universal appeal. Owners talk of the Bora today as though it were still being built, and this quite rightly is reflected in the model's second-hand value. A low-mileage, mint-condition Bora is a Maserati to keep, although not easy to find.

In fact, the Bora is considered one of the very best of all mid-engine exotics. It was quiet, comfortable, roomy and very fast. With great handling and excellent feel it is hard to imagine anyone not falling in love with the Bora. Current prices are no longer low; Boras and Ghiblis are both excellent investments. About the only drawback to the Bora is that it is difficult to work on due to the mid-engine configuration.

Engine
Type:. . . . . Bora (V-8)
Bore x stroke, mm/inches: 93.9x85, 3.8x3.4
Displacement, cc:. 4719
Valve operation:. . . . . four overhead camshafts
Compression ratio: 8.5:1
Carburetion: . . . . four 42DCNF Webers
Bhp (factory): . . . . 310@6000 rpm
Chassis & Drivetrain
Clutch: . . . . single dry plate
Transmission: 5-speed
Rear suspension: . . . . coil spring,
            hydraulic shock absorber
Front suspension: . . . . coil spring,
            hydraulic shock absorber
Frame: . . . . .integral chassis/body unit
General
Wheelbase, mm/inches: 2600, 104
Track, front, mm/inches:. 1474, 58.9
    rear, mm/inches: 1447, 57.8
Brakes:. . . . . .disc
Tire size, front and rear: 215/70 VRx15
Wheels:. . . . . light alloy disc
Coachbuilder: . . . . Oficine Padane
Note: Offered with the 4900 cc V-8 engine from 1976 on. All US cars were 4.9 standard after 1972.

Typical of a Giugiaro design—functional and compact. The Bora
delivered with ease everything its looks promised.

Viewed from the rear with twin exhaust tail pipes emerging
through the grille beneath the bumper. This style of rear bumper
did not conform to the USA import laws.

Bora pluses were perfect seating and instrument layout, with good visibility; poor-quality carpeting, center console and bulkhead materials were minus points. Location of the hand brake was not popular.

This is all you can see of the Maserati V-8 engine beneath the large air filter housing. Toward the rear, under the cover, is the spare wheel.

CHAPTER 15
MERAK
1972-1981

The Maserati tradition of creating a new car around one of its already existing engines was again illustrated at the Paris Salon in 1972. The Merak, also styled by Ital Design, was powered by the three-liter V-6 engine, which in 2.7-liter configuration had been used in the Citroën SM. Since the V-6 was a compact unit, two tiny seats were placed in the rear of this steel-bodied coupe, although they are of no practical use for adults.

There was a definite change in quality control with this new Maserati, for the interior and exterior finish were not up to Maserati's usually high standards. Whether this was restricted to the initial production versions is not known, but certainly the paintwork, leather and trim came in for heavy criticism from first-time owners.

With a lighter weight than the Bora, the Merak was a nimble, mid-engine GT with excellent roadholding. The Citroën hydraulics were still incorporated in the design, although from 1978 on the factory reverted to a normal braking system.

From 1972 until the end of 1975, some 1,300 Meraks were sold, including right-hand-drive models. This was a high-volume output for the Modena factory.

The Merak became the SS in 1975 when the first upgraded version was exhibited at Geneva. This revised Merak was 100 pounds lighter; larger carburetors and increased compression helped the V-6 produce an additional 30 bhp. Wheel and tire sizes became the same as on the Bora, with changed suspension settings and a more even weight distribution.

Several Merak SS's were sold in 1976, although serious production did not commence until a year later. By the close of 1978 almost 250 examples of the SS had been built.

With an eye toward the home market, De Tomaso offered a two-liter Merak in late 1976. The Merak 2000 was built for the Italian consumer, since a new tax on engine capacities above 2000 cc was to become law. However, the Merak 2000 had a short life and faded from the catalog in 1981, the model name being represented solely by the SS.

The Merak was not one of Maserati's most successful cars; perhaps because its qualities were overshadowed by the Bora, or because it came at a difficult time in the factory's history. The engine was a flier, though, and typical of Maserati design in that it loved to run at a high rpm; but in the final analysis it was not loved like the V-8.

At a quick glance the Merak looked very similar to the Bora; this is a 1974 Merak at the Maserati factory.

Though the quick and nimble Merak is a lot of fun to drive the V-6 does not provide the same kind of excitement as the Bora. Plus there are reliability problems with the early timing chains—there is an after-market kit that converts the tensioning mechanism to a more reliable system. Later Meraks, particularly the SS, seemed to be of much higher quality finish throughout.

With prices currently running slightly less than the Bora, the Merak does presently look like a good investment, although long term.

Engine
Type: .... Merak (V-6)
Bore x stroke, mm/inches: 91.6x75, 3.7x3
Displacement, cc: 2965
Valve operation: .... four overhead camshafts
Compression ratio: 8.75:1
Carburetion: .... triple 42DCNF Weber
Bhp (factory): .... 190@6000 rpm
Chassis & Drivetrain
Clutch: .... single dry plate
Transmission: 5-speed
Rear suspension: .... coil spring,
hydraulic shock absorber
Front suspension: .... coil spring,
hydraulic shock absorber
Frame: ....integral chassis/body unit
General
Wheelbase, mm/inches: 2600, 104
Track, front, mm/inches: 1474, 58.9
rear, mm/inches: 1447, 57.8
Brakes: ....disc
Tire size, front and rear: 185 VRx15, 205 VRx15
Wheels: .... light alloy disc
Coachbuilder: .... Ital Design
Note: Merak SS, introduced in 1975, developed 220 bhp @ 6500 rpm. Merak 2000, introduced in 1976, V-6 engine with bore x stroke 80x66.3 inches, 1999.6 cc, developed 159 bhp @ 7100 rpm.

Interior of the SS; sadly, the quality did not improve. Heating and ventilating was totally revised and instruments were neatly angled toward the driver.

The SS version of Maserati's Merak shows a grille on the hood, the deep air deflector beneath the nose and the wider-section tires. Outwardly these were the only alterations.

Forward of the rear subframe is the wonderful V-6 Maserati SS
engine, but the visual impact is of an untidy conglomeration of
belts, pipes and cables.

The two cast-aluminum flying struts at the rear leave the louvered
engine cover exposed. Unlike the Bora, the Merak had no rear
glass panel.

Seen here at the Turin show in 1976; the Merak 2000 was built by Maserati exclusively for sale in Italy.

CHAPTER 16
BITURBO
1982-ON

Shown to the press in December 1981, the Biturbo was a new concept for production motor cars, and a revelation for Maserati. It offers a unique combination of a V-6 two-liter engine with two inlet valves per cylinder operated by a single camshaft with a single turbo compressor on each bank. This light alloy unit in twin turbo form delivers 180 bhp at 6000 rpm, and will propel the car from 0-62 mph in 6.5 seconds with a claimed maximum speed of over 130 mph.

At the time of this writing, it is too early to know how this Maserati will be received, but in Italy, at a price of thirteen million lire, orders presently outstrip supply. Maserati dealerships around the world are eagerly awaiting their quotas.

Certainly, for a two-door four-seater sports coupe, the Biturbo has plenty to offer, but its place in the market will be alongside BMW, Mercedes and Jaguar. Only time will tell if De Tomaso has got it right, which will enable the name of Maserati to be projected toward a certain future.

The Biturbo has been available in the US as of early 1984. It is very quick with a larger 2.5-liter engine putting out 190 horsepower. It should also be quite nimble and fun to drive. For 1984, a four-door version should be available in Europe. The tradition of gorgeous interiors has been maintained. With the acceleration of a Porsche 928 and a mid-twenties price, the Biturbo should do well in America.

Engine
Type: . . . . Biturbo (V-6)
Bore x stroke, mm/inches: 82x63.5, 3.2x2.5
Displacement, cc: 1996
Valve operation: . . . . twin overhead camshaft
Compression ratio: 7.8:1
Carburetion: . . forced by two IHI turbo compressors
Bhp (factory): . . . . 180@6000 rpm
Chassis & Drivetrain
Clutch: . . . . single dry plate
Transmission: . . . . 5-speed or automatic
Rear suspension: . . . . coil spring,
hydraulic shock absorber

Front suspension: . . . . coil spring,
hydraulic shock absorber
Frame: . . . . integral chassis/body unit
General
Wheelbase, mm/inches: 2514, 100.5
Track, front, mm/inches: 1420, 56.8
rear, mm/inches: 1431, 57.2
Brakes: . . . . disc
Tire size, front and rear: . . . . . 195/60 HR14 Pirelli P6
Wheels: . . . . light alloy disc
Coachbuilder: . . . . Maserati factory
Note: 2.5-liter, 190 horsepower in US version.

Interior of the Biturbo is luxurious with leather and corduroy upholstery and walnut fascia.

The 1982 Maserati Biturbo displays a wedge shape with clean, unobtrusive lines.

There is adequate room and comfort for rear
passengers in this two-door coupe.

The familiar oval badge, now with white background, is mounted
on the trunk instead of the hood. Spare wheel is slung beneath
the undertray.

The exciting Maserati V-6 Biturbo engine.

The Biturbo chassis/body unit is produced in a new factory at De Tomaso's Innocenti premises. From this factory in Turin the Biturbo is transported to Modena for completion.

The 420/420 S was introduced in December 1985 as a two-liter version of the 425, with identical measurements. Fuel injection became available after December 1986. The two-liter engine now had an output of 185 hp, and the 2.5 liter with Katalysor output 177 hp.

First shown as a two-liter at the 1984 Turin Motor Show, the body was designed and made by Zagato. The Spyder had different dimensions: wheelbase 2400 mm/96 inches and length 4040 mm/ 161.6 inches. Zagato designed a detachable hardtop in fiberglass resin that became available early in 1987.

The Karif, first seen at Geneva in December 1988, was a two-seater coupe. The engine was the 2.8 liter V-6 with twin water-cooled turbochargers and double intercoolers. Output was 285 hp @ 6000 rpm. Top speed was over 200 km/h, and it went 0-100 km/h in 4.8 seconds. The car had a short wheelbase of 2400 mm/96 inches, front track was 1500 mm/60 inches, rear track was 1475 mm/59 inches, and length was 4040 mm/161.6 inches.

2.24 v equals two liters, 24 valves. Spoilers and skirts show the differences between this new car and the earlier two-door models. The 1996 cc V-6 (bore and stroke 82 x 63 mm) has four ohc, four valves per cylinder and an output of 245 hp @ 6000 rpm. Wheelbase is 2515 mm/100.6 inches, front track is 1460 mm/58.4 inches, rear track is 1455 mm/58.2 inches, length is 4190 mm/167.6 inches, width is 1715 mm/68.6 inches, and height is 1305 mm/52.2 inches. Its top speed is 230 km/h and 0-100 km/h is reached in 5.9 seconds.

A6GCS 1947-1950 ★★★★

The A6GCS is generally referred to as the cycle-wing Maserati, owing to its body design, or the "Cyclops" because of its central spotlight mounted in the grille. Either is a universally accepted term to use when differentiating between this model and the Series II of the same title.

In the period 1947 to 1950 the factory constructed fifteen of these delightful road-racing cars, and in that context they proved very effective. The model's first appearance was on the circuit of Modena in September 1947, where they finished first and second.

The FIA's new Formula Two regulations came into force for the 1948 season, and, consequently, the A6GCS received little factory attention.

All the cycle-wing engines were of single cam two-liter design, except the last one, serial number 2019, and mated to a four-speed Maserati gearbox. The engine proved very reliable, discounting an initial series of weak oil pipes strangely peculiar to the first two or three engines, and simple for the private owner to maintain. To the Italian race spectator this A6GCS was not an uncommon sight at speed events, road races and hill climbs up to the early fifties. However, the factory was not looking for volume sales and so the model was a rare sight outside its home country.

All examples were left-hand drive, and the model cost two million lire when new. Like many competition cars after their era has passed, these sports racing cars drifted into obscurity and only had an extended lifespan in South America, where some were used until the power unit expired beyond hope. It is known for certain that four survive, all in Europe, with unsubstantiated rumors of an additional three examples still intact.

If you ever have the opportunity to drive an A6GCS, seize it, for the model is the epitome of all sports racing cars of its time. The ride is hard and the road-holding mostly by guesswork, but if driven quickly they can be enormous fun and still controllable.

SERIAL NUMBERS
2001 to 2012 inclusive
2014, 2016, 2019

Engine
Type:................................A6GCS
Bore x stroke, mm/inches: 72x81, 2.9x3.2
Displacement, cc:............................1978
Valve operation:........ single overhead camshaft
Compression ratio: 11:1
Carburetion: ....triple 36 or 38 DO4 Weber
Bhp (factory): .... 130@5200 rpm
Chassis & Drivetrain
Clutch: .... single dry plate
Transmission: 4-speed
Rear suspension: .... leaf spring,
hydraulic shock absorber

Front suspension: .... coil spring,
hydraulic shock absorber
Frame: .... tubular
General
Wheelbase, mm/inches: 2310, 92.4
Track, front, mm/inches:................. 1225, 49
rear, mm/inches: 1160, 46.4
Brakes:................. aluminum drum, iron liner
Tire size, front and rear: 5.50x16
Wheels:....... Borrani wire, center-lock, knock-off
Coachbuilder: .... Medardo Fantuzzi

The A6GCS, driven by Alberto Ascari, pictured at the start of the Modena sports car race in September 1947.

One of the surviving cycle-wing Maseratis pictured in 1981 during its return visit to the factory in Modena. This is serial number 2014, which raced in the 1951 Grand Prix of Rome driven by Adolpho Schwelm.

A6GCM 1951-1953 ★★★

A direct descendant of the cycle-wing was this single-seater racing car built to comply with the new Formula Two regulations of 1952.

The prototype was completed in April 1951 with a tubular chassis, not dissimilar to the 4CLT, and the two-liter single cam engine from the A6GCS. It was not a very original combination and the car's roadholding was nonexistent. Before the end of 1951, two almost identical cars were finished and handed over to the Scuderia Bandeirantes. Development work was continued by engineer Massimino right up to the 1952 Italian Grand Prix, by which time the engine had undergone major design alterations. The power unit had identical bore and stroke dimensions of 75 mm, but now with gear-driven twin camshafts, revised porting and the fitting of 45DC03 Webers.

The next phase in the model's development came with the arrival of Gioachino Colombo, as a replacement for Massimino. Colombo redesigned the chassis and rear suspension and carried out more engine improvements in readiness for 1953.

Finally, Maserati had its competitive Formula Two car and with it ably attacked the Ferrari stronghold.

The final specification of the A6GCM revealed a potent two-liter racing car of good proportions with pleasant appearance and apparently it was not a difficult machine to drive at its limits. If nothing else, it served to illustrate to Omer Orsi that progressive development and testing of race cars could lead to a winner.

SERIAL NUMBERS
2032 to 2038 inclusive
2041, 2044, 2046, 2048, 2051

Engine
Type: A6GCM
Bore x stroke, mm/inches: 76x72, 3x2.9
Displacement, cc: 1978
Valve operation: . . . . twin overhead camshaft
Compression ratio: 13:1
Carburetion: . . . . .triple 40 DC03 Weber
Bhp (factory): . . . . 190@7000 rpm

Chassis & Drivetrain
Clutch: . . . . multi dry plate
Transmission: 4-speed
Rear suspension: . . . . leaf spring,
hydraulic shock absorber
Front suspension: . . . . coil spring,
hydraulic shock absorber
Frame: . . . . tubular

General
Wheelbase, mm/inches: 2310, 92.4
Track, front, mm/inches: 1225, 49
rear, mm/inches: 1160, 46.4
Brakes: . . . . aluminum drum, iron liner
Tire size, front and rear: 5.25x16, 6.50x16
Wheels: . . . . Borrani wire, center-lock, knock-off
Coachbuilder: . . . . Medardo Fantuzzi

The Italian Grand Prix on September 7, 1952, with Froilan Gonzalez on his way to a second place with the A6GCM Maserati.

The great Juan Manuel Fangio driving the factory-entered A6GCM to its first major win at Monza in 1953. The model is shown in its final form with the ultimate engine specifications.

A6GCS 1953-1955 ★★★★

The lessons of ignoring sports car racing by not giving the cycle-wing Maseratis due attention were rectified with the A6GCS Series II. Using as a basic design the rear suspension and engine from the Formula Two car, although in a considerably more civilized state of tune, Omer Orsi instructed his designers to create a competition sports car capable of performing well in endurance racing.

At the end of 1952, prior to the appearance of the new model, number 2040, a one-off A6GCS was constructed. This car was a transition between cycle-wing and all enveloping styles. It was an indication of factory intent to cope with the new sports car regulations that effectively banned cycle-wing design.

The first showing of the Series II sports racing A6GCS, which was also labeled A6GCS/53 or Sport 2000, was in the 1953 Mille Miglia. Instantly, there was little doubt that Maserati had produced a very capable sports car.

Good race results came its way for the remainder of 1953 and all through 1954 and 1955. The car had excellent acceleration and manageable roadholding, was totally reliable and a certain winner in its class. Many Italian sports car drivers "cut their teeth" on this model.

In appearance the A6GCS was a small, well-proportioned conventional sports car with undeniably attractive lines, completely curved, with no aspect obtrusive—typical of the Italian school. The visual impression of the body laying between the wheels was enhanced by its overall low build and high, sweeping front wings. The air intake received one of two design treatments, either vertical aluminum rods or large central motif. On some examples the passenger compartment was sealed off with a metal tonneau cover.

For some years the A6GCS has been quietly sought after; so today it is rarely offered on the market. The survival rate is high, almost sixty percent of the factory's total production.

SERIAL NUMBERS

2039, 2040, 2042, 2043, 2045, 2047, 2049, 2050
2052 to 2062 inclusive
2064 to 2093 inclusive
2096 to 2099 inclusive

Engine
Type: A6GCS
Bore x stroke, mm/inches: 76.5x72, 3.1x2.9
Displacement, cc: 1985.6
Valve operation: . . . . twin overhead camshaft
Compression ratio: 9:1
Carburetion: . . . . triple 40DCO3 Weber
Bhp (factory): . . . . 170@7300 rpm
Chassis & Drivetrain
Clutch: . . . . multi dry plate
Transmission: 4-speed
Rear suspension: . . . . quarter-elliptic springs,
hydraulic shock absorber
Front suspension: . . . . coil spring,
hydraulic shock absorber
Frame: . . . . tubular
General
Wheelbase, mm/inches: 2310, 92.4
Track, front, mm/inches: 1335, 53.4
rear, mm/inches: 1220, 48.8
Brakes: . . . . aluminum drum, iron liner
Tire size, front and rear: 6.00x16
Wheels: . . . . Borrani wire, center-lock, knock-off
Coachbuilder: . . . . Medardo Fantuzzi, Celestino
Fiandri, Pinin Farina (4 cars)

The interim A6GCS Maserati, serial number 2039, was delivered to the New York auto show in January 1953. Its parentage, both the cycle-wing and Series II models, can clearly be seen.

At the 1953 Turin motor show, two A6GCS's were exhibited: serial numbers 2040 and 2042. Note the grille style on both examples.

250F 1954-1958 ★★★★★

To compile a short note on this classic Maserati racing car is more difficult than writing its full history. It was built to contest the new Grand Prix formula for unsupercharged 2½-liter capacity, which came into force in January 1954. The multitube space frame was designed by Valerio Colotti, who was also responsible for the transaxle used in conjunction with the de Dion and transverse leaf spring rear suspension. Initially the six-cylinder Formula One engine developed 240 bhp and eventually climbed to 270-275 bhp at revs in excess of 8000.

From day one the Maserati 250F looked like a Grand Prix winner, although a little overweight. Certain weaknesses in transmission and engine lubrication came to light through its initial venture, but by the start of the 1954 European season, there was a steady flow of customers. Unlike Ferrari, Maserati management encouraged the sale of all competition cars to private teams and individuals. During that first year some ten 250F's were sold at an original price of just over 5,000 pounds sterling.

By the close of 1954, the 250F had won two world championship races. It was obvious that the car had all the speed of its rivals plus good handling, and was not complicated to look after.

Changes and development continued apace for the 250F. The five-speed transaxle came in 1955, as did a single-bore exhaust pipe, thinner-gauge chassis tubing, more engine power and improved ducting.

Experiments during the life of the model embraced a fully aerodynamic body, direct fuel injection, disc brakes, modified cylinder head using 10 mm spark plugs and eventually a V-12 engine from the design of engineer Alfieri. The improvements culminated in Fangio winning the 1957 World Championship with the 250F, scoring forty points. Maserati's great rival, Ferrari, scored not one championship race win.

At the end of that season many followers thought the factory would continue into 1958 with the twelve-cylinder version of the 250F, but it retired. It was with considerable regret that Omer Orsi closed the racing department with the exception of some mechanics to assist the privateers.

The factory built twenty-nine examples of this racing car, and upgraded to Grand Prix specification four of the A6GCM cars. The 250F was the epitome of a Formula One car of its period with Vanwall, Mercedes-Benz, Ferrari and Lancia its rivals—in all but looks. It will forever remain a firm favorite of motor racing enthusiasts everywhere.

SERIAL NUMBERS
2501
2505 to 2509 inclusive
2511 to 2516 inclusive
2518 to 2534 inclusive
2502, 2503, 2504, 2510 were uprated Formula Two frames

Engine
Type: 250F
Bore x stroke, mm/inches: 84x75, 3.4x3
Displacement, cc: 2493
Valve operation: twin overhead camshaft
Compression ratio: 12:1
Carburetion: triple 45DC03 Weber
Bhp (factory): 270@8000 rpm
Chassis & Drivetrain
Clutch: multi dry plate
Transmission: 5-speed in unit with axle
Rear suspension: de Dion, transverse leaf spring, hydraulic shock absorber

Front suspension: coil spring, hydraulic shock absorber
Frame: tubular
General
Wheelbase, mm/inches: 2280, 91.2
Track, front, mm/inches: 1300, 52
rear, mm/inches: 1250, 50
Brakes: aluminum drum, iron liner
Tire size, front and rear: 5.50x16, 6.50 or 7.00x16
Wheels: Borrani wire, center-lock, knock-off
Coachbuilder: Medardo Fantuzzi

Fangio drifting at high speed on his way to second place in the 1957 Italian Grand Prix at Monza. It was the finest year of the 250F.

Jean Behra at the Modena autodrome during 1957, trying out the latest modifications to a works 250F Maserati. The testing of race cars at the autodrome was a necessary and frequent task.

150S 1955-1957 ★★★

This was the first four-cylinder engine that was built under Omer Orsi's management.

The 150S project was begun in early 1954 under the direction of engineer Bellentani; from the outset it lacked positive definition and urgency. The first new 1½-liter engine was put into a power boat in October 1954.

With the project under the direction of engineer Alfieri, the 150S was eventually completed by April 1955. It was observed that the roadholding and handling of this first model was not without its problems, and considerable suspension modifications were done. The chassis was comprised of oval-section tube with round-section outriggers and boxed-front cross section. The rear suspension utilized a de Dion tube with transverse leaf spring located beneath the tube. The triangle for lateral location and stability, used to good effect on the A6GCS, was placed on top of the 150S differential. The differential casing, cast in either aluminum or elektron, did suffer in its racing life from considerable stress, resulting in fracture. The model's debut, however, erased all the delays and problems associated with its design: Jean Behra won the Nürburgring 500 km race in late August 1955.

More alterations to the frame resulted in the wheelbase being increased 100 mm and the rear triangle being eliminated, but the transverse spring was stiffened.

The chassis, without modification, was used by many privateers to house the two-liter version of the four-cylinder engine; and some had a five-speed gearbox installed.

By the end of 1957 a 150S convertible had been built, using an A6GCS rear axle, clutch and gearbox. The coachwork was created by Fantuzzi and the serial number was 150G.T.-03. It finally left the works in March 1960. Although described in factory documentation as a berlinetta and Gran Touring car, it was in truth a right-hand-drive spyder. Possibly intended as a prototype for a limited production run, the project was beset with problems and, therefore, remained a prototype.

It is difficult to know how many 150S sports cars remain in their original form, for they were updated by many owners for the 2000 cc racing class. The four-cylinder engine has an important significance in Maserati history, since it was the basis of the 200S and, later on, the motive power for the Birdcage.

SERIAL NUMBERS
1650 marine installation
1651 to 1657 inclusive
1659 to 1675 inclusive

Engine
Type: 150S
Bore x stroke, mm/inches: 81x72, 3.2x2.9
Displacement, cc: 1484
Valve operation: ....twin overhead camshaft
Compression ratio: 9:1
Carburetion: .... twin 45DCO3 Weber
Bhp (factory): .... 140@7500 rpm

Chassis & Drivetrain
Clutch: .... multi dry plate
Transmission: 4-speed
Rear suspension: ... de Dion, transverse leaf spring, hydraulic shock absorber

Front suspension: .... coil spring, hydraulic shock absorber
Frame: .... tubular

General
Wheelbase, mm/inches: 2200, 88
Track, front, mm/inches: 1250, 50
rear, mm/inches: 1200, 48
Brakes: .... aluminum drum, iron liner
Tire size, front and rear: 5.25x16, 5.50x16
Wheels: .... Borrani wire, center-lock, knock-off
Coachbuilder: ....Celestino Fiandri, Medardo Fantuzzi

The 1956 version of the 150S Maserati chassis.

The first right-hand-drive four-cylinder sports racing car from the factory in postwar times—certainly a clean, aerodynamic shape.

200S/200SI 1955-1957 ★★★

It was Maserati's intention to cope with the competition from Ferrari's 500 Mondial with a two-liter sports racing car of similar specification to the 150S. The transition could have been easy and relatively inexpensive but, of course, there were problems; not the least of which was the factory commitment to Grand Prix racing.

Initially a two-liter engine was put straight into a 150S frame by the Tony Parravano team for the 1955 Targa Florio. At the same endurance race the factory entered a 200S, albeit with rigid rear axle.

The first appearance of a true 200S did not take place until the Tour of Sicily early in April 1956.

By June of the same year a lighter 200S chassis had been built with a longer and lower body shell. The car was fitted with a five-speed gearbox and entered in the Supercortemaggiore Trophy race at Monza.

Feedback racing the 200S to the factory from drivers agreed the model was very fast but its handling was suspect. Even with a de Dion rear end, the 200S was not a popular car with the Italian road racing fraternity. In addition, they had fond remembrances of the handling of the A6GCS, and were hopeful that Maserati could develop the 200S in the same way.

The factory continued to build and enter the two-liter car in all manner of sports car races throughout Europe in 1955 and 1956.

The sports car regulations changed for 1957 and required the fitting of a top, full-width windshield, windshield wipers and minimum-size doors on both driver and passenger side. The factory carried out these modifications, designating the new model 200SI.

Many examples were sold to American customers, and they were successful over a two-to-three-year period. For a sports racing car, total output was high at thirty-three completed cars, which included both the S and SI variants.

SERIAL NUMBERS
2401-2433 inclusive

Engine
Type: 200S, 200SI
Bore x stroke, mm/inches: 92x75, 3.7x3
Displacement, cc: 1993
Valve operation: . . . . twin overhead camshaft
Compression ratio: 9:1
Carburetion: . . . . twin 45DCO3 Weber
Bhp (factory): . . . . 186@7500 rpm
Chassis & Drivetrain
Clutch: . . . . multi dry plate
Transmission: . . . . 4- or 5-speed
Rear suspension: . . . de Dion, transverse leaf spring,
hydraulic shock absorber
Front suspension: . . . . coil spring,
hydraulic shock absorber
Frame: . . . . tubular
General
Wheelbase, mm/inches: 2200, 88
Track, front, mm/inches: 1250, 50
rear, mm/inches: 1200, 48
Brakes: . . . . aluminum drum, iron liner
Tire size, front and rear: 5.50x16, 6.00x16
Wheels: . . . . Borrani wire, center-lock, knock-off
Coachbuilder: . . . . Celestino Fiandri,
Medardo Fantuzzi

The Maserati 200S as seen at Monza in 1956.

A customer's 200SI all ready to leave the factory for delivery to the USA.

250S 1957-1958 ★★★

The origins of the 2½-liter sports car began with the 1954 Supercortemaggiore race when Maserati entered two right-hand-drive A6GCS's, with 2500 cc six-cylinder engines. In reality the power unit was a Grand Prix 250F engine utilizing milder camshafts and valve timing, and lower compression pistons.

The location for right-hand steering on the A6GCS chassis would not have been a difficult modification, although the de Dion rear end with four-speed transaxle necessitated some tube cutting.

The two cars were driven at Monza but no further competition appears to have been done with these "specials." Today one engineless example languishes in Italy in a forlorn state. Two engines to this specification were supplied to Automobiles Talbot for its 1956 Le Mans attempt.

The 2½-liter four-cylinder Maserati used the 200S cylinder block, bored out and with new crankshaft and other internals, in a basic 200SI frame. Consequently, the 250S looked little different externally from a 200S; the only difference was in the engine output, which increased another 10-12 bhp. The debut of this new model was, like so many other new Maseratis, at the 1,000 km race in Buenos Aires in early 1957.

The factory built a total of four "pure" 250S cars—in other words, 2½-liters, not uprated 2000 cc versions. There is no record of their competition history, if indeed they had any, and no reliable source to confirm the serial numbers. However, number 2432 was a 250S consigned to Carroll Shelby Sports Cars, Inc., in August 1958.

Engine
Type: 250S (4-cylinder)
Bore x stroke, mm/inches: 96x86, 3.8x3.4
Displacement, cc: 2489
Valve operation: . . . . .twin overhead camshaft
Compression ratio: 9.75:1
Carburetion: . . . . twin 45DCO3 Weber
Bhp (factory): . . . . 198@7800 rpm
Chassis & Drivetrain
Clutch: . . . . multi dry plate
Transmission: 5-speed
Rear suspension: . . . de Dion, transverse leaf spring,
hydraulic shock absorber
Front suspension: . . . . coil spring,
hydraulic shock absorber
Frame: . . . . tubular
General
Wheelbase, mm/inches: 2200, 88
Track, front, mm/inches: 1250, 50
rear, mm/inches: 1200, 48
Brakes: . . . . aluminum drum, iron liner
Tire size, front and rear: 5.50x16, 6.00x16
Wheels: . . . . Borrani wire, center-lock, knock-off
Coachbuilder: . . . . Medardo Fantuzzi

The 1954 Maserati 250S based on the six-cylinder engine.

Serial number 2432, a genuine 250S Maserati with four-cylinder engine, built in 1958.

300S 1955-1958 ★★★★★

The three-liter version of Maserati's Grand Prix engine, installed in a new chassis with Grand Prix front and rear suspension, bode well for the 1955 Sports Car Championship. Although not as powerful as the 250F engine, the 300S was aptly suited to sports car events, with appropriate gear ratios in the four-speed transaxle.

Unusual was the sale of three examples to Briggs Cunningham almost before the factory had raced its own team of cars.

The 300S was a popular competition Maserati with many private teams, and demands for its quick delivery came from all over the world, especially from the U.S.A. The car had good handling qualities, reasonable acceleration and felt "very safe" to those who drove it. The car had a good career in the 1956 Sports Car Championship, but still finished second to Ferrari (six points behind).

During 1957 several works-entered 300S's were fitted with larger front drums from the 450S. The drivers felt it would increase braking efficiency and allow later braking into the corners, thus decreasing their lap times. Also, one or two of the factory cars had the more-acceptable five-speed transaxle.

It was apparent, looking at the events in which the 300S competed, that the car had racing stamina, and certainly its reliability was rarely in doubt. It just did not receive the factory development that could have turned it into an outright winner. Of the twenty-nine cars built it is known that nineteen still exist. Each is considered a sought-after sports racing car with a good pedigree, built during a period when the factory had tremendous enthusiasm for its motor racing.

SERIAL NUMBERS
3051 to 3074 inclusive
3076, 3077, 3080, 3082, 3083

Engine
Type: 300S
Bore x stroke, mm/inches: 84x90, 3.4x3.6
Displacement, cc: 2991
Valve operation: . . . . twin overhead camshaft
Compression ratio: 9:1
Carburetion: . . . . triple 45DC03 Weber
Bhp (factory): . . . . 280@7000 rpm
Chassis & Drivetrain
Clutch: . . . . multi dry plate
Transmission: . . . . 4- or 5-speed
Rear suspension: . . . de Dion, transverse leaf spring,
hydraulic shock absorber
Front suspension: . . . . coil spring,
hydraulic shock absorber
Frame: . . . . tubular
General
Wheelbase, mm/inches: 2310, 92.4
Track, front, mm/inches: 1300, 52
rear, mm/inches: 1250, 50
Brakes: . . . . aluminum drum, iron liner
Tire size, front and rear: 6.00x16, 6.50x16
Wheels: . . . . Borrani wire, center-lock, knock-off
Coachbuilder: . . . . Medardo Fantuzzi

A 1955 Maserati 300S. Note the air scoops within the grille mesh; the later model had them cut into the aluminum body beneath the lamps.

Harry Schell driving the 300S he shared with Stirling Moss to record second place at Sebring in March 1957.

350S 1956-1957 ★★★★

Searching for more cubic capacity and greater horsepower than the current straight-six three-liter was capable of giving, Maserati engineers decided to build this sports racing car with an early version of the production 3½-liter engine. In retrospect this idea may seem strange, but it saved considerable tooling costs and there wasn't another adaptable power unit available.

The initial experiments were to place a dry-sump version of the chain-drive twin overhead camshaft production engine in a tubular chassis which was to have housed a V-8 unit. Immediately it could be seen that the model was a conglomeration of ideas that was to meet with little success, mainly due to the paniclike thinking of the management, and the poor preparation.

The first car had the five-speed 300S transaxle with de Dion axle and the same suspension detail as the three-liter car. It suffered from severe handling problems and there was little time to sort out the car's roadholding.

Engineers realized the chassis was too heavy and the rear suspension, while proving satisfactory on the 300S, created steering problems during braking and acceleration. In fact, it was noted that the car had high-speed handling problems even in a straight line! The prototype was dismantled and later converted to a 450S; the 350S project received a revised frame, new front and rear suspension, and 450S-style transaxle. In tests, this 350S proved to be a different car.

The final 350S was constructed in late 1956 and entered in the Argentine 1,000 km race at Buenos Aires in January of the following year. Upon the car's return to Modena, a V-12 engine of 3500 cc was installed.

Of the three originally built, the prototype and number two survive with Maserati enthusiasts. The 350S was not the greatest sports racing car built at Modena, but the factory never gave it the testing and development program that was necessary.

SERIAL NUMBERS
3501 (later renumbered 4501)
3502, 3503

Engine
Type:...................... 350S (6-cylinder)
Bore x stroke, mm/inches: 86x100, 3.4x4
Displacement, cc:............................3483
Valve operation:..........twin overhead camshaft
Compression ratio: 9.8:1
Carburetion: .... triple 45DC03 Weber
Bhp (factory): .... 290@6000 rpm
Chassis & Drivetrain
Clutch: .... multi dry plate
Transmission: 5-speed
Rear suspension: ... de Dion, transverse leaf spring,
                        hydraulic shock absorber
Front suspension: .... coil spring,
                        hydraulic shock absorber
Frame: .... tubular
General
Wheelbase, mm/inches: 2325, 93
Track, front, mm/inches:................. 1300, 52
      rear, mm/inches: 1260, 50.4
Brakes:............... aluminum drum, iron liner
Tire size, front and rear: 6.00x16, 7.00x16
Wheels:........ Borrani wire, center-lock, knock-off
Coachbuilder: .... Medardo Fantuzzi

The 12-cylinder version of the 350S Maserati.

Awaiting the start of the 1957 Mille Miglia, the 3½-liter V-12, serial number 3503.

450S 1957-1958 ★★★

Probably the fastest sports car to emerge from the Maserati factory, the 450S was more than a match for the V-12 Ferrari engine in terms of power. Unfortunately, the model came at a time when its potential could not be developed fully, owing to serious financial constraints within the company. Its competition life must be viewed in that light.

The output from the ninety degree racing V-8 was over 400 bhp, with maximum power between 6800 and 7200 rpm. Acceleration was little short of nerve-shattering. A factory mechanic noted at the time that 0-100 mph in less than eleven seconds was quite impressive. But that was nothing compared with the acceleration from 100 to 170-plus mph! As can be imagined, the noise from this brutish sports car was deafening, and if heard from a distance sounded like rolling thunder. Visually it was a lot larger than the 300S, and the original aluminum blisters and protrusions disappeared after the prototype to give a clean, aerodynamic contour.

In preparation for the 1957 Mille Miglia, engineer Colotti designed a two-speed supplementary gearbox which was located between engine and transaxle. In practice it worked on the principle of an overdrive reducing the load on the engine without affecting terminal speed. This development was incorporated in the fourth of the 450S Maseratis built.

Problems in racing the 450S were in fact few, for the powerful V-8 engine, transmission and chassis gave little trouble, possibly because of its robust design. The brakes were always overworked during a race (not surprising when you realize the speed and size of the car) and consequently did suffer from fatigue, especially on demanding, tight circuits.

Both of the works 405S cars were crashed in Caracas and with the FIA imposing a three-liter limit on the Sports Car Championship for 1958, the management's announcement of withdrawal from motor racing came as little surprise.

The 450S was one of the great sports racing cars, born in an era when big, front-engine roadsters were in vogue. It is remembered today with affection and respect.

SERIAL NUMBERS
4501-4510 inclusive

Engine
Type:..................................... 450S
Bore x stroke, mm/inches: 93.8x81, 3.8x3.2
Displacement, cc:...........................4477
Valve operation: .... four overhead camshafts
Compression ratio: 9.6:1
Carburetion: .... four 45IDM Webers
Bhp (factory): ....400-420@7500 rpm
Chassis & Drivetrain
Clutch: .... multi dry plate
Transmission: 5-speed
Rear suspension: .... transverse leaf spring,
                                 hydraulic shock absorber
Front suspension: .... coil spring,
                                 hydraulic shock absorber
Frame: .... tubular
General
Wheelbase, mm/inches: 2400, 96
Track, front, mm/inches:.................. 1350, 54
        rear, mm/inches: 1300, 52
Brakes:................ aluminum drum, iron liner
Tire size, front and rear: 6.00x16, 7.00x16
Wheels:....... Borrani wire, center-lock, knock-off
Coachbuilder: .... Medardo Fantuzzi

The fabulous Maserati V-8 racing engine of 1957, which developed in excess of 400 bhp.

The Maserati 450S with Jean Behra in control during development tests in April 1957.

Tipo 60 1959-1960 ★★★★★

With the urge for motor racing in his blood, and engineering expertise still very much available within the factory, Orsi gave his consent for the low-key construction of another two-liter sports racing car. It was thought this would keep the Maserati name in front of home market buyers and possibly reflect on sales of its 3500GT production car. The two-liter racing class in Italy during this period was of primary interest to most manufacturers.

The design theme for the Tipo 60 was lightness, and in this respect engineer Alfieri scored maximum points and advanced far ahead of the competition. His chassis consisted of approximately 200 thin tubes of varying diameters from 10 to 15 mm welded together to form a strong, lightweight frame. Steel plates were used for mounting engine, suspension and transmission. The finished car, when seen by American motoring journalist Karl Ludvigsen, was aptly described as, "a near infinite number of tubes of near infinite thinness." It was known in Italy as the spaghetti racer, but generally the nickname Birdcage was adopted, and today is accepted as defining this model.

The two-liter engine was developed from the four-cylinder 200S block. The cylinder head was a new design, as was the curved, finned crankcase. The latter was a result of forming a triangular shape on the underside of the engine so that the unit could be frame-mounted at forty-five degrees. Obviously the hood height was as low as possible for a front-engine car, and even with the dry-sump oil tank mounted alongside, the profile remained unspoiled. The rear end was of the Kamm design.

The Birdcage was intended as a customer's car for the two-liter class of racing and was extremely popular in America where it won a wide variety of events. The car had superb handling and braking characteristics, light steering and speed—with an ideal power-to-weight ratio. Its only weakness was the chassis frame; its rigid design required constant checking for cracks or fractures. Such maintenance paid dividends, for a Birdcage chassis damaged in a race was just a pile of tubing, with precious little that could be salvaged.

Today, the Tipo 60 is held in high regard by enthusiasts of sports car racing. Those who have an intimate knowledge of the Birdcage consider it to be the ultimate development of its class and design.

SERIAL NUMBERS

2451, 2460, 2462, 2465, 2466, 2468

Engine
Type:.............................60 (Birdcage)
Bore x stroke, mm/inches: 93.8x72, 3.7x2.9
Displacement, cc:..............................1989
Valve operation:...........twin overhead camshaft
Compression ratio: 9.8:1
Carburetion: ....twin 45DCO3 Weber
Bhp (factory): ....200@7800 rpm
Chassis & Drivetrain
Clutch: .... multi dry plate
Transmission:............................5-speed
Rear suspension: ... de Dion, transverse leaf spring, hydraulic shock absorber
Front suspension: .... coil spring, hydraulic shock absorber
Frame: .... tubular
General
Wheelbase, mm/inches: 2200, 88
Track, front, mm/inches:................. 1250, 50
       rear, mm/inches: 1200, 48
Brakes:................................disc
Tire size, front and rear: 5.50x16, 6.00x16
Wheels:........ Borrani wire, center-lock, knock-off
Coachbuilder: .... Gentilini and Allegretti

The hammered aluminum skin of the prototype Tipo 60 Maserati.

Stirling Moss testing the prototype two-liter Birdcage at the Modena autodrome in May 1959.

Tipo 61 1959-1961 ★★★★★

This was the 2.9-liter version of the Tipo 60 and was built and raced alongside its sister model. The first requests for a more powerful Birdcage came from America where it was felt the car could be a serious competitor and win a Sports Car Club of America championship.

The original chassis underwent little modification other than strengthening the de Dion tube, hub carriers and transaxle casing. The power unit, however, had considerable development. The crankshaft and connecting rods were more robust to cope with the increase in bore and stroke. The 100 mm bore for the 2900 cc four-cylinder block was the very limit that the casting could accommodate; consequently, the cylinder liners were extremely thin. After engineer Alfieri had sorted the internals, the engine developed a reliable 250 bhp.

For Le Mans 1960, there were three Birdcage Maseratis, all with different body styles. One had a high-profiled windscreen almost sixty inches long; another had a long, sweeping tail; and the third had a completely standard style.

The car's potential was never fully realized in European racing, since the factory had neither the funds nor time to go motor racing. Preparation and development of the Tipo 61 were given to the Camoradi team, which was also short of money. The model's history was in America where, driven by an assortment of professional and amateur drivers, results were good and plentiful for two seasons.

By the end of the 1961 season, yet another replacement Birdcage was under development. This hastened the demise of the front-engine three-liter version which, like the Tipo 60, was regarded as the ultimate sports car of its time.

SERIAL NUMBERS
2451 (converted from a Tipo 60)
2452 - 2459 inclusive
2461, 2463, 2464, 2467, 2469, 2470, 2471, 2472

Engine
Type: ....61 (Birdcage)
Bore x stroke, mm/inches: 100x92, 4x3.7
Displacement, cc: 2890
Valve operation: ....twin overhead camshaft
Compression ratio: 9:1
Carburetion: ....twin 48DC03 Weber
Bhp (factory): .... 250@7000 rpm

Chassis & Drivetrain
Clutch: .... multi dry plate
Transmission: 5-speed
Rear suspension: ... de Dion, transverse leaf spring, hydraulic shock absorber
Front suspension: .... coil spring, hydraulic shock absorber
Frame: .... tubular

General
Wheelbase, mm/inches: 2200, 88
Track, front, mm/inches: 1250, 50
     rear, mm/inches: 1200, 48
Brakes: .... disc
Tire size, front and rear: 5.50x16, 6.00x16
Wheels:........ Borrani wire, center-lock, knock-off
Coachbuilder: .... Gentilini and Allegretti

This overhead shot of the Tipo 61 streamliner at Le Mans illustrates the length of the windscreen and the good proportions of this Birdcage. Chuck Daigh, the American driver, is about to do his share of the driving.

The Tipo 61 rebodied by Piero Drogo in 1962 was raced by Casner during that year and 1963 without success.

Tipo 63/64 1961-1962 ★★★★

Alfieri set to work on the design of a rear-engine Birdcage before the end of 1960. He had thoughts of using a V-8 3000 cc engine, but completed his design using the Tipo 61 engine mounted in the chassis at an angle of fifty-eight degrees. This new rear-engine sports car was on the test track by mid-December 1960; there were grave doubts about the roadholding and steering. The Tipo 63 chassis was essentially the same as that of the Tipo 61 Birdcage, but with independent rear suspension and two fuel tanks located laterally the correct weight distribution was critical. On the test car it was obvious that more development work on steering and suspension was desperately needed.

The Tipo 63 was competitive and basically strong, since it had survived on tortuous, demanding circuits. However, the factory had already decided to install a potent V-12 Maserati engine into the rear of a Tipo 63, which was accomplished by April 1961. The former 250F Formula One power unit developed around 320 bhp.

The Tipo 64, which appeared in the winter of 1961-62, was a revised Tipo 63 with de Dion rear end, improved front suspension and a V-12 engine. The problems of factory participation in motor racing were probably highlighted with this model more than any other. The factory relied heavily on teams such as Cunningham and Serenissima. But while these teams were both willing and capable, there was no real development or back-up from the factory. Once the new model was built, sold and delivered it was almost as though Orsi sighed with relief that some profits had materialized; it was no way to go chasing a world championship title.

SERIAL NUMBERS

63002, 63004, 63006, 63008 (four cars constituted total output of both Tipo 63 and Tipo 64)

Engine
Type:.........................63/64 (Birdcage)
Bore x stroke, mm/inches: 100x92, 4x3.7
Displacement, cc:...........................2890
Valve operation:..........twin overhead camshaft
Compression ratio: 9.8:1
Carburetion: .... twin 48IDM Weber
Bhp (factory): .... 260@7000 rpm
Chassis & Drivetrain
Clutch: .... multi dry plate
Transmission: 5-speed
Rear suspension: .... coil spring,
                          hydraulic shock absorber
Front suspension: .... coil spring,
                          hydraulic shock absorber
Frame: .... tubular
General
Wheelbase, mm/inches: 2200, 88
Track, front, mm/inches:................. 1225, 49
       rear, mm/inches: 1200, 48
Brakes:................................. disc
Tire size, front and rear: 5.50x16, 6.00x16
Wheels:........ Borrani wire, center-lock, knock-off
Coachbuilder: .... Gentilini and Allegretti
Note: The V-12 engine had a bore and stroke of 70.4x
      64 mm. developed 320 bhp@8200 rpm. Optional
      was the fitting of light alloy disc wheels.

The cockpit of a Tipo 63, similar to the front-engine Birdcage. The multiplicity of tubes is apparent.

The former Scuderia Serenissima rear-engine Tipo 63 Maserati Birdcage, serial number 63004.

Tipo 151 1962-1965 ★★★★

The FIA regulations in 1962 for the Sports Car Championship were designed to encourage manufacturers of G.T. cars back into competition. The Maserati factory had nothing eligible, so promptly designed and constructed a front-engine coupe powered by the former 450S V-8 engine. The substantial chassis was built of oval and round tubing, with five-speed transaxle and a strange three-piece de Dion tube expected to cope with the power. The engine was, in effect, from a 450S, but with reduced capacity so it could race within the four-liter G.T. prototype class at Le Mans.

The prototype 151 was duly tested and found to have a high terminal speed and reasonable handling, although the transaxle arrangement was of some concern. The fastest 151 coupe recorded a speed of 177 mph on Mulsanne, and was obviously a lot quicker than the Ferraris.

Engineer Alfieri installed the engine from the 5000GT model in the French team's 151, suitably modified with fuel injection yet retaining the wet sump. The rear suspension underwent improvements and a normal de Dion tube was installed. This became the 151/1. For stage two of the 151/1's development and redesign, a new chassis was built, the 5000 cc engine was dry-sumped with new injection equipment and a new lower, wider body shell was fitted. The coupe, now 151/3, was blindingly fast and recorded a speed of 191 mph on the Le Mans straight.

With further chassis and suspension modifications carried out by the factory during the winter, the revised coupe was tested satisfactorily in Italy and appeared at Sebring for practice where it crashed, damaged beyond repair and killing Lucky Casner.

SERIAL NUMBERS
151:002 (renumbered 151/1, 151/3, 151/4)
151:004, 151:006

Engine
Type:....................................151
Bore x stroke, mm/inches: 91x75.8, 3.6x3
Displacement, cc:...........................3943
Valve operation:.......... four overhead camshafts
Compression ratio: 9.7:1
Carburetion: .... four 45IDM Webers
Bhp (factory): .... 360@7000 rpm
Chassis & Drivetrain
Clutch: .... multi dry plate
Transmission: 5-speed
Rear suspension: .... coil spring,
                                    hydraulic shock absorber
Front suspension: .... coil spring,
                                    hydraulic shock absorber
Frame: .... tubular
General
Wheelbase, mm/inches: 2300, 92
Track, front, mm/inches:............... 1250, 50
      rear, mm/inches: 1280, 51.2
Brakes:................................... disc
Tire size, front and rear: 6.00x16, 7.00x16
Wheels:........ Borrani wire, center-lock, knock-off
Coachbuilder: .... Allegretti
Note: The five-liter engine had a bore and stroke of
      94x89 mm and developed 430 bhp @ 7000 rpm.

The handsome 151 coupe pictured June 14, 1962, prior to its Le Mans debut.

The 1964 version of the 151 coupe owned by Maserati-France on the Montlhéry bank during the 1,000 km race.

Tipo 65 1965 ★★★

Development of the Tipo 65 Maserati was prompted by the accident that killed Casner in Colonel Simone's 151 coupe, which left the team without a 1965 Le Mans entry. With financing promised by Colonel Simone, engineer Alfieri created the Tipo 65 around a Birdcage chassis that was a mixture of types 63 and 64. The engine was, as used in the last coupe, a fuel-injected five-liter with five-speed transaxle bolted to it, all rear mounted. The finished car was not beautiful.

For the twenty-four-hour race, the Tipo 65 was to be driven by Jo Siffert with Jochen Neerpasch. Although they had little time to familiarize themselves with the new car, they each achieved some respectable lap times; but both complained of front-end wandering for no apparent reason. The car lasted a few laps before Siffert hit a bank that resulted in total water loss. It was retired and returned to Modena, where the chassis was revised and some new bodywork made. The Tipo 65 was later sold to a car-racing enthusiast in Europe.

The Tipo 65's life was certainly brief and without glory, and it was the last Maserati sports racing car built.

SERIAL NUMBER
151:002 (as for the 151/4 coupe)

Engine
Type: 65
Bore x stroke, mm/inches: 95x89, 3.8x3.6
Displacement, cc: 5046
Valve operation: .... four overhead camshafts
Compression ratio: 9:1
Carburetion: .... fuel injection
Bhp (factory): .... 430@7000 rpm
Chassis & Drivetrain
Clutch: .... multi dry plate
Transmission: 5-speed
Rear suspension: .... torsion bar, hydraulic shock absorbers
Front suspension: .... coil spring, hydraulic shock absorbers
Frame: .... tubular
General
Wheelbase, mm/inches: 2400, 96
Track, front, mm/inches: 1400, 56
     rear, mm/inches: 1370, 54.8
Brakes: .... disc
Tire size, front and rear: 6.00x15, 6.50x15
Wheels: .... Borrani wire, center-lock, knock-off
Coachbuilder: .... Allegretti

Not particularly handsome with its long, flat tail; it was painted in Maserati-France colors of white with red and blue stripes.

The Tipo 65 Maserati photographed behind the factory, before its delivery to Le Mans.

MASERATI PRICES 1981-1983

This was a particularly difficult section to compile, for a number of reasons. If a Maserati is sold for a considerably higher price than the model is currently valued at, it is extremely difficult to get confirmation of such a figure from either the buyer or seller, for understandably personal reasons. Also, it is a problem trying to record asking and selling prices when there is no central store of information about such Maserati activities.

What has emerged during the past three or four years of buying and selling Maserati production cars is that each in its own way is on the increase and none has taken a hesitant step in the steady increase in value. There are a number of Italian exotic cars that positively skyrocketed to high prices only to falter or even drop within a year. That is what we call fashionable buying, and for some totally unaccountable reason it has never affected the Maserati market. If anything, for a number of years Maserati prices lay dormant and the Maserati was truly the unfashionable Italian car to own. We would offer the opinion that since 1980 the situation has altered, with good effect for the owners and potential buyers.

As a guide to current trends in the buying and selling market, we have used the classified sections of the bimonthly magazine of the Maserati Information Exchange (*Via Ciro Menotti*) over the past twelve issues. This has particular relevance to the American Maserati market, since it would be pointless incorporating European prices by merely converting pounds or lire into dollars.

Keep in mind that a left-hand-drive Ghibli convertible, for example, has a higher value in the USA than in Europe; conversely, a Bora or Khamsin to Europeans possibly has a higher value.

Do not shop around for your Maserati purchase by sticking exclusively to the following prices, but use them as a guide and their worth will be apparent.

MASERATI PRICES 1984-1989

The upward trend over the past five years has continued; Maseratis are progressively more expensive to buy now because more potential buyers are in the marketplace and good examples of the marque are rarely offered for sale.

An excellent 3500GTI coupe just realized $60,000 at a European public auction, an example of its upward spiral. The price chart following should be used as a guide only.

	High Price	Average Price	Low Price
3500GT/3500GTI/3500GTIS coupes			
1981	$ 6,000	$ 4,500	$ 1,500
1982	10,500	4,500	4,500
1983	15,000	8,000	4,500
1989	60,000	40,000	25,000
3500 Vignale spyder			
1981	7,500	6,000	3,000
1982	13,000	7,500	3,500
1983	17,500	8,500	6,000
1989	150,000	80,000	60,000
3500/3700/4000 Mistral coupes			
1981	7,500	6,000	4,500
1982	10,500	7,500	6,000
1983	15,000	10,500	6,000
1989	70,000	42,000	30,000
3500/3700/4000 Mistral spyder			
1981	12,000	6,000	3,500
1982	20,000	10,500	6,500
1983	24,500	13,000	8,000
1989	150,000	80,000	60,000
Quattroporte			
1981	6,000	4,500	3,000
1982	7,500	6,000	4,500
1983	10,500	7,500	4,500
1989	25,000	18,000	12,000
Mexico			
1981	6,000	4,500	3,000
1982	9,000	6,000	4,000
1983	15,000	8,000	5,500
1989	30,000	24,000	15,000
Ghibli			
1981	16,000	8,000	4,500
1982	19,000	12,000	6,000
1983	22,000	14,000	8,000
1989	100,000	60,000	40,000
Ghibli spyder			
1981	20,000	16,000	10,000
1982	35,000	25,000	15,000
1983	45,000	35,000	20,000
1989	300,000	200,000	100,000
Indy			
1981	6,000	6,000	4,500
1982	9,000	7,500	4,500
1983	12,000	10,500	6,000
1989	60,000	35,000	25,000
Bora/Khamsin			
1981	17,500	12,500	7,500
1982	20,000	12,500	10,500
1983	21,500	15,000	10,500
1989	80,000	45,000	40,000

Eliminated are incomplete cars and those with incorrect engines or accident damage.

RECOMMENDED MASERATI BOOKS

Maserati Road Cars: The Postwar Production Cars 1946-1979 by Richard Crump and Rob de la Rive Box. Published by Osprey Publishing Ltd., 1979.

Maserati: Sports Racing & GT Cars From 1926 by Richard Crump and Rob de la Rive Box. First published 1975; second edition published by Haynes Publishing Group, 1983.

Maserati: A Complete History From 1926 to the Present by Luigi Orsini & Franco Zagari. Published by Libreria dell'Automobile, 1982.

Maserati: The Postwar Sports Racing Cars by Joel E. Finn. Published by John W. Barnes Publishing, 1977.

Maserati Birdcage by Joel E. Finn. Published by Osprey Publishing Ltd., 1980.

Maserati: A History by Anthony Pritchard. Published by David & Charles Ltd., 1976.

Maserati 250F by Denis Jenkinson. Published by Macmillan Ltd., 1975.

Maserati Owner's Handbook by Hans Tanner. Published by Floyd Clymer Ltd., 1961.

Il Tridente by Severo Boschi. Published by Editoriale il Borgo, 1970.

Maserati, Lamborghini, Iso, de Tomaso by Shizuo Takashima. Published by Car Graphic Library, 1977.

Maserati Pocket History by Gianni Cancellieri and Cesare de Agostini. Published by Libreria dell'Automobile, 1981.

Maserati G.T.: Car of the Connoisseur by M. M. Schwartz. Published by Maserbook, 1976.

Vittorie 1926-1954. Compiled and published by the Maserati factory, 1955, with contributions from various sources.

Maserati 1965-1970. Compiled by R. M. Clarke. Published by Brooklands Books Ltd.

Maserati 1970-1975. Compiled by R. M. Clarke. Published by Brooklands Books Ltd.

Maserati Bora & Merak by Jan P. Norbye. Published by Osprey Publishing Ltd., 1982.

The Maserati 250F by Anthony Pritchard. Published by Aston Publications, 1985.

Maserati 3011 by Denis Jenkinson. Published by Aries Press, 1987.

Maserati Catalogue raisonne 1926-1984. Published by Automobilia, 1984.

Rivista Maserati 1 edited by Bruno Alfieri. Published by Automobilia, 1985.

Maserati Biturbo by Stefano Pasini. Published by Automobilia, 1986.

Maserati Dalle Origini Al Biturbo. Compiled by E. Golinelli and A. Ferrari. Published by Edizioni Rebecchi, 1985.